'B

Václav Řepa is a professor of Informatics at the University of Economics, Prague and at the PanEuropean University in Bratislava. He is specialized in the methodology of information systems development, project management, and business processes modeling and management. For last two decades his research activities are aimed on the relationship between the business process management and information systems development.

He is an establishing member and the presidency member of the Slovak Association for Process Management (SAPRIA) and the establishing member and the president of the Committee of Guarantors of the Central European Association for Business Process Management (CEABPM)

Information Modeling of Organizations

selected chapters

by prof. Václav Řepa

ℬ

2012

Published in the Czech Republic by Tomáš Bruckner, Řepín – Živonín, 2012
Academic Series

This publication was reviewed by doc. Ing. Ján Závadský, PhD., The Faculty of Economics, Matej Bel Universtiy, Banská Bystrica, Slovakia.

Acknowledgement: The work presented in this book has been supported by the Czech project GAČR 402/08/0529 Business Process Modelling.

Paperback printed on demand and worldwide distributed by Lightning Source UK Ltd. Pitfield UK and Lightning Source Inc. La Vergne TN US. New prints are available for ordering in every bookstore.

Visit us at http://pub.bruckner.cz

ISBN 978-80-904661-3-5

CONTENTS

FOREWORD

This book is about the information modeling of organizations. The term Information Modeling, as is usual in the field of informatics, generally, has several different meanings. This book uses the concept in the *widest sense possible*. It does not express just the Information System, nor the **technological** view of the organization. In fact it represents the *general meaning of the term "organizational modeling" with the light flavor of informatics practices*. Informatics practices influence this conception of organizational modeling in two main ways:

- Although the topic of the cognition of organizational structure and behavior regularities traditionally belongs under management theory; informatics brings to this area the necessary precision in the shape of formal specifications and a systemic style of thinking. Informatics is a source of sophisticated techniques and tools, like conceptual data modeling, for example, aimed at discovering the general regularities of the organizational structure and behavior (often called "business rules"). Also, the ability to abstract all the non-contentual (non-informational) aspects of the (organizational) system is a strong tool for the essential precision of the cognition.

- Information technology is a key enabler of organizational changes as it is established in all literature mentioning the theory of reengineering (see *Hammer M., Champy J. (1994) "Reengineering the Corporation: A Manifesto for Business Evolution", Harper Business, New York,* for instance). Consequently, the well designed Information System must be a clear picture of all the significant aspects of the organization (both the structural and the behavioral ones). Information modeling aims to create the view of the organization which is, on the one hand independent of any non-contentual aspect (including the infor-

mation technology, at first); on the other hand, it is fully consistent with following the process of the development of the
Information System (i.e., the infrastructure in general), and
thus it can be regarded as the first step in this procedure.

The book consists of five chapters, each of them is relatively independent of the other. Nevertheless together they form one consistent
text. Each chapter has its own localised numbering of figures and tables. The content of a chapter represents the specific topic connected
to the topics of the other chapters.

The **first chapter** introduces the reader to the topic of Business System Modeling. It mentions the underlying principles and explains the
principle of the two-dimensional view of the business system. It also
references the formal Business Modeling Specification as the common
basis for all views of the organization occurring in the following chapters.

The **second chapter** focuses on the behavioral aspects of the organization. It describes the MMABP methodology for the business processes analysis and design, as well as the Process Diagram technique
for the description of the business process run. This chapter also explains all general principles, mentioned in the preceding chapter, in
detail.

The **third chapter** deals with the problem of the coherency of different models. It explains the coherency as a root of the model's quality, and introduces the concepts of completeness and correctness.
Specific attention is paid to the question of "structural coherency" as
the very deep level of the methodology support of the process of cognition.

The last two chapters elaborate the business process view of the organization.

The **fourth chapter** describes the methodical procedure of the
building of the process managed organization based on the general
concept of "service orientation".

The **fifth chapter** describes the specific features and general consequences of the business process management in the area of public
administration.

1. Business Systems Modeling

This chapter describes the systemic approach to the modeling of the business system based on the formal business metamodel. It has been developed as a result of several years of research in the area of business process modeling at the Prague University of Economics. The main products, and other important aspects of the research, are described in Repa V., Matula M. (2002), as well as in my older papers (see references).

The first subchapter roughly describes the general principles of the modeling of the business. It also identifies and defines the concept of "conceptual modeling" and the principles behind it.

Based on those principles, the next subchapter states the general view of the topic of conceptual modeling in the context of the object oriented paradigm. It discusses the particular possibilities and restrictions of the Unified Modeling Language (UML) in the sense of making the conceptual object model. It also identifies the substantial need for linking particular tools, as well as the need for the general principles of such linking.

The next subchapter increases the concept of conceptual modeling to two dimensions, and discusses the necessity of covering both dimensions by specific tools with specific principles and rules. The importance of linking these two dimensions together is also discussed in this chapter.

The last subchapter describes the contents of the formal business metamodel based on the UML metamodel and is described by means of it.

The conclusion contains a brief summary and outlines the future work in the sense of the main topic of this chapter.

1.1 Modeling the Business System

The crucial basic principle of the Information System's (IS) development is the **Principle of Modeling**.

This principle expresses the presumption that the *objective basis for the implementation of the business system in the organization must be constituted by real facts existing outside of, and independently of, the organization.* Such real facts are considered as relevant, which substantially influence the possibility of the organization to achieve its objectives. These facts are visible in the form of specific (critical) values of so-called critical factors. Each real world object, playing any important role in the business system, we can model as a collection of attributes expressing those critical factors. We call them **business objects**. Critical changes in the critical factor values are recognized as (external) events. Events are regarded here as the only reason to start the **business process** – the process trigger[1].

In the area of business processes, the principle of modeling states that the system of the business processes in the organization is the model of relationships between objectives and critical events, and mutual relationships between the objectives and between the events. The purpose of each business process in the organization is to ensure the proper reaction for any given event. Essential relationships between the organization's objectives, critical factors and events are expressed in the form of relationships between particular processes. Products of those processes, as well as their actors, goals, problems, circumstances and other aspects should correspond to the relevant business objects.

The purpose of the principle of modeling in the area of business modeling is:

- it defines the basis for the analysis (what is the **essential substance** to be analyzed);
- it leads to creation of such a **system of business processes** which:
  - is able to react to each significant change requiring also change in business processes (changes of goals, objectives and critical factors);

---

[1] The concept of events is very wide here – it covers even such changes of facts which are not usually regarded as "changes of critical factors values". For example, customer requests, or changes of production technology parameters are also regarded here as events (i.e. "critical" changes).

- is optimal – it consists of all processes, and only those, which are necessary under the given business conditions.

The Information System, as an infrastructure for the business system, has to be based on the same objective model of the real world. Such an objective model of the real world is traditionally called the **conceptual model**.

The concept "conceptual" was, at first, used in the area of data modeling. It expresses the fact that the database should describe the essential characteristics of the real world: **objects and their mutual relationships**.

There are three mutually dependent main principles which together explain the sense and the reason for the term "conceptual":
- The Principle of Modeling,
- The Principle of Three Architectures, and
- The Principle of Abstraction.

From the data point of view, the contents and the structure of database objects reflect the contents and structure of the real world objects. Correctness of the data model is measured via its similarity to the real world. In order to make such measurements, the term "similarity" must be defined exactly. Therefore, the special tool – Entity Relationship Diagram (ERD) has been developed (Chen P. P. S. (1976)). The ERD describes the essential characteristics of the real world: objects and their mutual relationships. It is constructed to be able to describe exactly the objects and their relationships in the same way as we see them in the real world. At the same time, this model describes the essential requirements for the database – it must contain the information about the same objects and their relationships. The form in which the particular database describes these facts always depends on the technological and implementation characteristics of the environment in which the database is realized. But the essential shape of the model still remains the same. Because of the need to describe the same database in its various shapes (essential, technological, implementational) the principle of different architectures has been formulated. This principle, generalized to the scope of the whole system (not only its database), we call **"The Principle of the Three Architectures"** (see Repa V. (1999a)).

The Principle of the Modeling proves to be general, too –some parts of the system processes also have to be regarded as the model of the real world. But the main problem of the so-called structured approach in the IS's development is that it is not able to recognize which system processes form the model of the real world, and which do not. Such recognition requires separation of the modeling operations from the others and organizing them into the special algorithms according to real world objects and their relationships. And this point of view is not attainable under the "structured paradigm" without accepting the natural unity of the modeling system processes and the data in the database. Acceptance of the natural unity of the modeling processes and the data entities, formulated as the main OO principle enables us to solve Yourdon's problems with control processes (see Yourdon, E. (1989)) – the essential controlling algorithms follow on from the entity life histories.

As shown above, the Modeling Principle seems to be general and independent of existing paradigms. Each new paradigm can only specify its place in IS development but cannot eliminate or limit it.

The Principle of Abstraction expresses the fatal need for creating abstract concepts while modeling the real world. There are many possible classifications of abstractions. Undoubtedly, **hierarchical abstractions** are very important kinds of abstraction.

Hierarchical abstractions are the means for breaking down the elements of the designed Information System to the level of detail. Higher level concepts consist of the lower level ones. On each level of detail, the elements of the developed IS, and their relationships are described. The elements on each higher (i.e. non-elementary) level of detail are abstract concepts. Only the lowest (i.e. most detailed, elementary) level contains definite elements. There is the "tree structure" of dependencies between the concepts of the higher and lower levels. This is so that each element has one 'parent' element on the higher level (with the exception of the highest element – the root of the tree), and can have several 'child' elements on the lower level (with the exception of the lowest elements – the leaves of the tree). Hierarchical abstractions are of two basic types:

- Aggregation. Subordinated elements are parts of the superior concept.
- Generalization. Subordinated elements are particular types of the superior concept.

The aggregation type of abstraction is typically used for breaking down processes – functions into sub-functions (using the Top-Down procedure), while the generalization type of abstraction is typically used for breaking down conceptual objects into sub-objects (specialization into object types). The incompatibility of these two basic approaches with the concept break-down forms the basis for a lot of problems and misunderstandings, not only in structured methods (it has often been a source of vital problems for the "structured paradigm"), but also in object-oriented methods.

All the three above mentioned main principles are generally explained in the following chapter "Modeling Enterprise Activities", the sub-chapter 2.2.

1.2 CONCEPTUAL MODELING UNDER THE OBJECT PARADIGM

As mentioned above, the "conceptual" concept was first used in the area of data modeling. This origin is still visible in the common understanding of the adjective "conceptual", in the sense of modeling with the standard tool for object-oriented modeling – the Unified Modeling Language (UML – see UML (2010)):

Object-oriented analysis and design materials, written by Craig Larman for ObjectSpace (www.objectspace.com), describe **conceptual modeling** as the following:
- Classes representing concepts from the real-world domain.
- Binary associations describe relationships between two concepts.
- The concepts can have attributes but no operations.
- General associations indicate that the specialized concepts are subsets of a more general concept. The specialized concepts have associations, or attributes, that are not in the general concept.
- Each association conclusion can have graphical adornments indicating their end name, multiplicity, and much more.

Cris Kobryn (Kobryn, C. (2000)), Co-Chair UML Revision Task Force, takes the conceptual model into account, speaking about the "Structural Model" as a view **of a system that emphasizes the structure of objects, including their classifiers, relationships, attributes and operations**. The purpose of such a model is to show the static structure of the system:
- the entities that exist,
- internal structure,
- relationship to other entities.

In addition, Kobryn gives several tips for structural modeling:
- Define a "skeleton" (or "backbone") that can be extended and refined as you learn more about your domain.
- Focus on using basic constructs well; add advanced constructs and/or notation only as required.
- Defer implementation concerns until later on in the modeling process.
- Structural diagrams should:
    - emphasize a particular aspect of the structural model;
    - contain classifiers at the same level of abstraction.
- Large numbers of classifiers should be organized into packages.

Roni Weisman (Weisman, R. (1999)) from Softera also speaks about the "Conceptual System Model". He distinguishes three types of objects:
- Entity (objects which hold the system's data),
- Boundary Object (interface objects which directly interact with the external world – actors),
- Control Object (objects which manage the system operations).

As may be seen from previous paragraphs, there are several approaches to conceptual modeling in the area of object-oriented methods. Each of them reduces the Object Model (represented by the Class Diagram) to the model of objects and the relationships between them, represented by their attributes, but not by their methods. This reduction is present also in Roni Weisman's approach (see above), even if he takes into consideration "Entities", as well as "Control Object". Just the fact of distinguishing between "static" and "dynamics ensuring" objects is the best demonstration of such a reduction. The common understanding of the term "conceptual" thus tends to the synonym for "static".

This article argues for the "really object-oriented" approach to conceptual modeling. At first it means that it is necessary to model not only the static aspects of the real world, but also its dynamics. The existence of the object as the collection of data (attributes) and functions (methods) is to be the right reason for data processing operations control (strictly speaking: the object life cycle). See Figure 1.1:

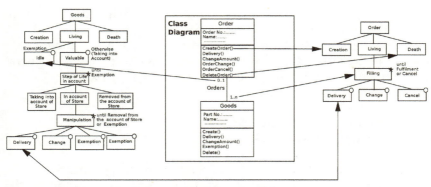

Figure 1.1. Object Life Cycles versus Object Model.

Regarding the conceptual point of view, together with the principles of object orientation, one must stop taking the object's methods just as a collection of procedures usable for communication with other objects. One should seek the wider – conceptual sense of them as a whole – search out the substance of their synergy. Such a "higher sense" of the object's methods represents the **object life cycle**.

Figure 1.1 illustrates the object life cycle as a complement to the Class Diagram. It can be easily seen that all methods of the conceptual object should be ordered into one algorithm which describes for each method its place in the overall process of the object's life. This place defines the conceptual sense of the method. In this sense it is obviously absurd to take into account such methods as "give_list" or "send_status", as well as it being absurd to speak of "sending messages" between objects (discussion between the Order and the Goods in this example). Such a point of view is suitable for the model of objects in a program system but in the case of conceptual objects it is clearly improper.

The figure also indicates the fact that there are dependencies between the methods of the different objects which correspond to the association between objects, not only in the sense of existence (method "Delivery" in this example), but also in the "structural sense" – in the sense of the structure of a life cycle. So, in this example, the fact that "Goods do not need to be ordered" (partiality of the association), corresponds to the possibility of the "idle living" of Goods. Similarly, the fact that "Goods may be ordered more times" (cardinality n of the association), corresponds to the cycle of the "filling" part of the life of the Order. In order to better understand structural dependencies in general, which itself is the best way to precisely define those OO conceptual modeling principles, see Jackson, M. A. (1982).

It seems that with the topic of conceptual modeling, there could come the "renaissance" of clearly correct and unambiguous general principles of structured programming, according to Jackson.

1.3 TWO BASIC DIMENSIONS OF THE REAL WORLD BUSINESS MODEL

According to the principle of modeling, the model of the IS must be based upon the model of the real world. By "real world" we mean the objective substance of the activities to be supported by the IS, and of the facts to be stored in the IS. This demand is only met in the "static" parts of the conceptual model in the traditional sense (i.e., in the data or object model of the reality). In the model of the system's behavior (behavioral UML diagrams, Use Cases etc.), we model the Information System's dynamics, rather than the dynamics of the real world. We model there not only the objects, but also the users, of the IS; not only information sources but also its targets. On the other hand, it is clear, too, that the way in which the IS should behave (and should be used), is substantial. It arises from the rules of the real world – from business activities which define the sense of the IS in the form of the business need for information. So the crucial question is: what are the substantial real world actions and processes to be modeled?

Some solution is offered by the object model (class diagram) itself. The model of the real world, as the system of objects encapsulating the data with appropriate actions, speaks not only about the data which the IS stores, but also about the actions with the data and their sequences (processes). The system of conceptual objects, and their interaction, models the part of the real world dynamics which follows from the nature of the objects (their life cycles) and their relationships. But it does not model that part of the real world dynamics which follows from the substance of the information need; - from the nature of the business.

So, there are two kinds of "dynamics" of the real world to be analyzed within the process of IS development:
- Dynamics of the real world objects and their relationships given by their conceptual nature (real world conditions and constraints),
- Dynamics of the business activities given by the conceptual nature of the business processes (business nature).

We may conclude from the previous paragraph that there are two basic orthogonal views of the "real world":

- The object view which emphasizes the **substance of the real world**,
- The process view that emphasizes the **real world's behavior** (see Figure 1.2).

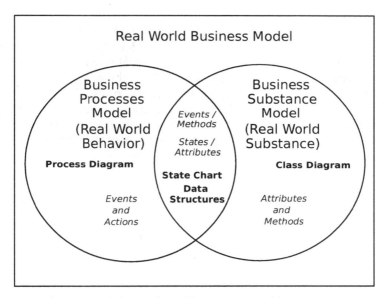

Figure 1.2. Two Parts of the Real World Business Model.

The first view (Business Substance Model), represents **objects and their mutual relationships** consisting of attributes and methods.

The second view (Business Process Model) represents **business processes** consisting of events and actions.

Of course, the model of objects also concerns their behavior in the form of entity life algorithms (method ordering). Such behavior is seen from the point of view of objects and their relationships. It says nothing about the main reasons for it. So, the **behavior of the objects should be regarded as the structural aspect of the real world**.

The significant aspect of the real world's behavior, seen from the process point of view; which is not present in the object point of view; is that there has to be a prime reason for the real world's behavior which is independent of the object life rules. In practice, it means that for each business process, some reason in the form of the goal, objective, and/or external input event (customer requirement), must exist. The business process as the collection of the actions, ordered by time, and influencing the objects (their internal states and their mutual behavior), is something more than just an amorphous collection of actions.

Similar to the structural modeling of the real world (Business Substance Model); even for the behavioral model (Process Model); it is necessary to describe the principles and general rules, and develop the tool (diagrammatic technique) which reflects them. Repa, V. (2000a), roughly states the basic principles and general rules of process modeling, and contains also the basic specification of the necessary diagrammatic tool – the Process Diagram – in the form of the Business Process Meta-Model. The following examples use the notation of that Process Diagram.

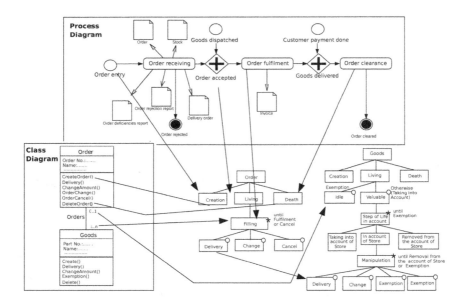

Figure 1.3. Relations between Process and Object Models.

Figure 1.3 illustrates how the process model explains the dependencies between objects and their life cycles, giving them a higher sense. This explanation is based on the perception of object actions in terms of the reasons for them – events and process states. Objects are playing the roles of attendees or victims (subjects), of processes. For completeness it is necessary to recognize the fact that one object typically occurs in more processes, as well as, one process normally combining the attendance of more objects. The orthogonality of those two points of view is also typical and substantial – it lends sense to this coupling. Structure and behavior is the analogy of the two basic dimensions of the real world – space and time.

Unfortunately, the Structure Diagram used for the description of the objects' life cycles at Figure 1.3 is not the regular diagram of the UML. The UML prefers an unstructured way of describing the context as it follows from historical circumstances.

Figure 1.4 illustrates the same as Figure 1.3 using the regular UML diagram – the State Diagram. It can be easily discerned that the difference between these two styles of precise description reflect the basic differences between the structured and unstructured views. In the structured view, there is the need for creating abstract higher units (such as "Living" and "Filling"). These units serve as a way of understanding the problem. Such a possibility is missing in the case of the State Diagram. On the other hand, the State Diagram allows for the reverse point of view of the object life cycle – in terms of states and the transitions between them. Such a view is very close to the position of the real attendee of the business (i.e., real world behavior), who usually sees the process in detail. A very serious problem is that this unstructured description often leads to the creation of subsidiary abstract concepts which have nothing to do with the real world (i.e., concepts which are not "conceptual"). In our example there is the problem with the presumption that the same event "Exemption" occurs twice, which is impossible in the real world. The reason for this is the impossibility of expressing the necessary combination of actions connected with this event in given situation (object state).

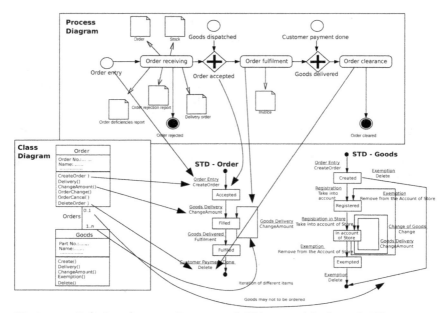

Figure 1.4. Relations between Process and Object Models through STD

Mutual dependencies among all Business System models, together with the methods of handling them, are explained in detail in chapter 3.

1.4 Business Modeling Specification

Business Modeling Specification (see Figure 1.5) consists of three associated packages:

- Business Substance MetaModel package
- Business Process MetaModel package
- Business Models Consistency package

Business substance and business processes represent two basic dimensions of the real world model mentioned in the previous text. Each of the two packages specifies the basic concepts required for a model of a given dimension together with the basic rules for expressing the business logic given by the dimension. As they are modeling the general basis of all possible models in a given dimension, they are both metamodels.

Unlike the other two packages, the Business Models Consistency package is not a metamodel to all intents and purposes. It models the general basis of the mutual interconnections and dependencies of both metamodels. In that sense, it extends both metamodels with new concepts in order to address the general mutual dependencies of the real world models.

The business substance model is based on the UML Class Model with minimal extensions. The business process model has its own rules that are not present in the current version of the UML. The consistency rules for both models are not present in the current version of the UML, either.

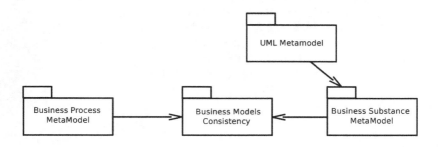

Figure 1.5. Business Modeling Specification Overview.

Business Substance MetaModel

The **Business Substance MetaModel package** (see Figure 1.6) specifies the basic concepts required for a model of a business substance, and defines the basic needs/possibilities of their mutual interconnections (i.e., business substance modeling logic – "how to model what the real world is").

It is based on the Core Foundation Package of the UML Metamodel (see UML (2010)), which it reduces, as well as extends, for the purpose of business substance modeling.

By this metamodel, the Core Foundation Package of the UML Metamodel is reduced to those concepts and constructions, which are relevant to the purpose of modeling the business substance. Such models are usually called "conceptual". Unfortunately, the term "conceptual" is closely connected with the term "static", which we regard as an improper reduction for the model of the real world, which is naturally dynamic (see previous sections).

Therefore, this metamodel also extends to the UML Metamodel with following concepts:

- The Class State as a subtype of the Behavioral Feature complements the concept Method. The purpose of its existence is to allow the taking of all the methods of a given class as an ordered whole in the time dimension. Such a chronologically ordered aggregate of actions is usually called an "algorithm". The algorithm structure of all methods of a given class is called the Class Life Cycle.

- The Class Life Cycle is the abstract name for the role of "Class" as an aggregate of the Class Life Cycle Steps.
  The Class Life Cycle Step is a collection of:
    - a possible one input state,
    - at least one output state,
    - possibly more processed attributes, and
    - one processing method.

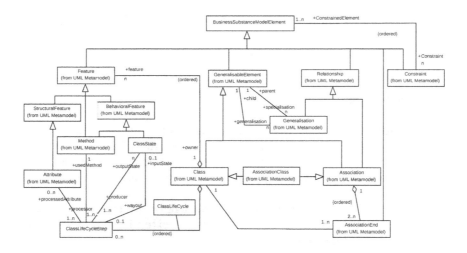

Figure 1.6. Business Substance MetaModel Package.

As "Class" is a generalizable element, so too should the Class Life Cycle, and the Class Life Cycle Step, inherit this feature. In practice, it requires the specification of general rules for generalizing algorithms, especially in the context of the consistency rules for both business models. At the current stage of our work, this topic has not been elaborated upon, as yet. We can find some inspiration in the work of M. A. Jackson, as was mentioned above (Jackson, M. A. (1975), Jackson, M. A. (1982)).

BUSINESS PROCESS METAMODEL

The Business Process MetaModel package (see Figure 1.7) specifies the basic concepts required for a model of a business process and defines the basic needs/possibilities of their mutual interconnections (i.e., business process modeling logic – "how to model; how the real world behaves").

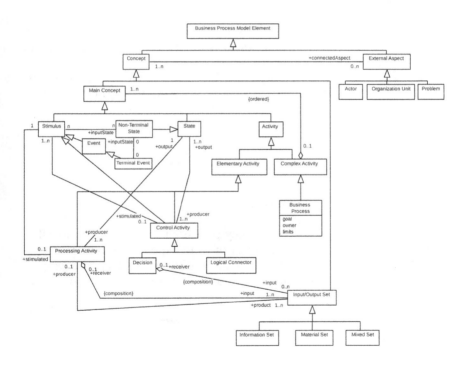

Figure 1.7. Business Process MetaModel Package.

- Control Activity as a Stimulus inherits the stimulation competence. Moreover, from the multiplicity 1 (i.e. monopoly) of the stimulation association follows that the Processing Activity can be stimulated either by the Event or the Control Activity exclusively.
- Each Stimulus has to have at least one input state, except for the very first Stimulus (Terminal Event), which has no input state. This exception is expressed by the specific zero-multiplicity association with the Terminal Event, which over-writes the inherited general association between the Stimulus and the Non-Terminal State.
- Each State has to be an input for at least one Stimulus, except the very last one (the Terminal State), which has no succeeding activity.
- The Characteristics of the terminal event, as well as of the terminal state, are relative to the specified model. Usage of the model as a part (sub-process) of another model will change all terminal events of the sub-process to regular ones and all terminal states to internal ones from the super-process point of view.
- The Processing Activity, as well as the Decision, is a composite aggregate of the Input/Output Sets. As it follows from that fact, one particular Input/Output Set can input either to the Decision, or to the Processing Activity, exclusively.

BUSINESS MODELS CONSISTENCY

The Business Models Consistency package (see Figure 1.8) specifies the basic rules required for models of both types to be mutually consistent. It uses the basic concepts from both metamodels, and extends them with new concepts and constructs required for the consistency specification.

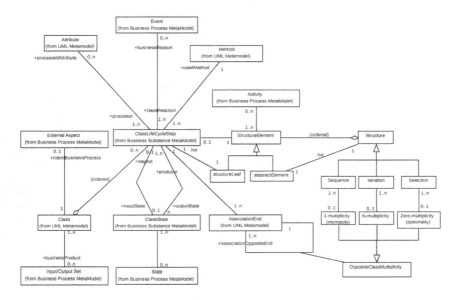

Figure 1.8. Business Models Consistency Package.

- To ensure "structural consistency" it is necessary to describe the class life cycle "in a structural manner". Therefore, this model extends the Business Substance MetaModel with the new concepts of: Structure, Structure Element, Structural Consistency Element, and Association Ends Couple.
- Each Class Life Cycle Step is a Structure Element, and as such, it is a part of the Structure. Structure is an ordered aggregation of Structure elements where each Structure Element is either a Structure Leaf or a Structure (as an Abstract Element) exclusively. Each Structure Element can, but does not have to, be, the Class Life Cycle Step, except for a Structure Leaf; which always must be in the Class Life Cycle Step. In the model, this is expressed by the non-optional association "isa", between the Structure Leaf and the Class Life Cycle Step, which overwrites the optional general association between the Class Life Cycle Step and the Structure Element.
- Structure must, and can only, be, one of the three types: Sequence, Selection, and Iteration.
- The abstract concept "Opposite Class Multiplicity" addresses the opposite end of each association of a given Class. This is necessary in order to associate it with the proper Structure

type (Iteration/Sequence/Selection) of the Structure Element describing the part of the Class Life Cycle.

Such a connection allows the expression of the structural correspondence between the association opposite end multiplicity, and the appropriate type of life cycle structure element:

- the multiplicity of each association opposite end requires at least one iteration in the class life cycle of a given Class;
- the monopoly of each association opposite end requires at least one sequence in the class life cycle of a given Class; and
- the optionality of each association opposite end requires at least one selection in the class life cycle of a given Class.

1.5 CONCLUSION

This chapter describes the systemic approach to the modeling of business systems based on the formal business metamodel. It arises from the belief that the main general principles underlying the idea of conceptual modeling (i.e., modeling, abstraction, and different architectures) are the best validation of such features of a language. At the moment this language has the form of a set of (meta)models.

In the near future, it will be necessary to complement the metamodels by a set of rules, and other tools, reflecting the main problems and challenges discussed above. For example:

- the completeness of the business process modeling rules
- the completeness of the business substance modeling rules
- the completeness of the consistency rules in the Models Consistency Model
- the problem of life cycle generalization

As a consequence of this evolution it is necessary to "put the metamodel into the business" in the form of a widely accessible and open tool for a generation of tools for business modeling based on this metamodel. This tool should also allow manipulation of the metamodel itself in order to facilitate its further evolution by interested parties. The above stated idea is the main topic of the "Open Soul Project" based on the principles of the work of "open source" communities. Such organization of work should allow the abovementioned further evolution of the metamodels by the community.

2. MODELING ENTERPRISE ACTIVITIES

This chapter describes the **methodology for analyzing business processes**. The methodology was developed at the Department of Information Technologies of the Prague University of Economics as a result of research, complemented by the experience gained from the twenty-month long series of activities (consisting of the realization of several projects) completed in summer 1997 at the Prague Energy Company. The first project had focused on requirements analysis in the area of human resources for the purpose of developing a HR Information System. The final report from the last project contained the roots of the methodology described in this chapter.

2.1 THE METHODOLOGY

The reasons for the development of the methodology are many and varied:

1. In the Information Systems development methodology *we need to identify the real substance of the activities to be supported by the IS*. At the conceptual level of system modeling, the model of the developed IS should be that of (what we call) "the real world". By the term "real world" we mean the real (objective, absolute) substance of the activities to be supported by the IS, and of the facts to be stored in the IS. This demand is only met in the "static" parts of the traditional conceptual model (i.e., in the data or object model of the reality). In the model of the system's behavior (functional model, Use Cases etc.) we model the Information System's dynamics rather than the dynamics of the real world. The model developed in the form of Data

Flow Diagrams, and/or Use Cases, is that of the IS's behavior rather than the clear conceptual real world behavior model. We model there not only the objects, but the users of the IS, too; not only the information sources, but also its targets. On the other hand, it is also obvious that the way in which the IS should behave (and should be used) is substantial – it arises from the rules of the real world – from those business activities which define the sense of the IS in the form of the business need for information. So, the crucial question is: what are the substantial real world actions and processes to be modeled? Some solution is offered by the object-oriented methods – the model of the real world as the system of objects encapsulating the data with the appropriate actions speaks, not only about the data which the IS stores, but also about the actions with the data and their sequences (processes). The system of conceptual objects (corresponding to the entities of the traditional conceptual data model); and their interaction; models that part of the real world dynamics which follows from the nature of the objects (their life cycles), and their relationships. But it does not model that part of the real world dynamics which follows from the substance of the information need; – from the nature of the business.

It seems that there are at least two kinds of "dynamics" of the real world to be analyzed within the process of IS development:

- the dynamics of the real world objects and their relationships given by their conceptual nature (real world conditions and constraints);
- the dynamics of the business activities given by the conceptual nature of the business processes (business nature).

Modeling the dynamics of the real world objects and their relationships is the main subject of OO Analysis Methodologies (Rumbaugh J., Blaha M., Premerlani W., Eddy F., Lorensen W. (1991), Coad P., Yourdon E. (1990)). We consider the Event Partitioning Approach proposed by Yourdon (Yourdon, E. (1989)) to be suitable for the conceptual modeling of the business processes. Also the convergence of these two approaches is to be the subject of interest (see Jackson, M. A. (1982), Repa V. (1995), Repa V. (1996)).

2. Additionally, in the area of the Business Processes Reengineering (BPR) theory, there is an actual need for the means (i.e. techniques, tools and methods) for identifying the substance of the processes to be (re)engineered. As the problem of BPR has a lot of dimensions, there is a number of approaches to BP analysis. These are: functionality, time-dependencies, value chains, financial flows, critical paths etc. (For analysis see Hammer M., Champy J. (1994), Greenwood R. M., Robertson I., Snowdon R. A., Warboys B. C. (1995), Scheer, A.–W. (1992), Scheer, A.–W. (1994)). But the common basis for all these approaches are the business processes themselves – their reasons, products, elementary activities and their sequences. Unfortunately, an exact approach to the BP analysis is still missing in this field, even though there is a number of a useful analogies with ISD methodologies and techniques.

3. Lately, the IT products supporting Workflow Management have become more and more interesting and useful. As a result of this fact, the need for the theory which answers the basic question "What is the origin of the workflow and where are the substantial rules for it to be looked for?" is becoming more and more relevant. Just as in the case of the BPR, also in this area an exact approach to the conceptual workflow analysis is still missing.

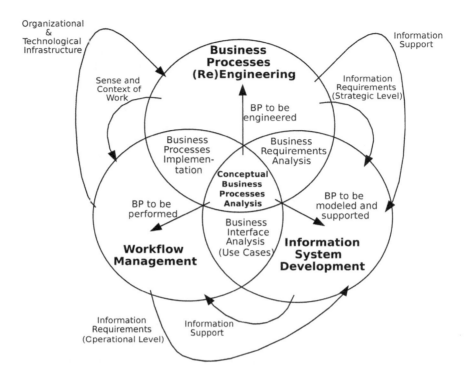

Figure 2.1. BPR vs. ISD vs. Workflow Management.

Figure 2.1 illustrates the convergence of BPR, Workflow Management and ISD. It presents the conceptual business processes analysis as the common basis for all three activities.

2.2 UNDERLYING PRINCIPLES

The methodology aims to create (i.e., analyze and design) a model of the system of the business processes which:
- respects the basic objectives and goals, current state and specific characteristics of the organization;
- respects the objective circumstances (those which are given outside of the organization and are independent of the organization) which can play a significant role in the behavior of the organization;

- is "optimal" in the sense of the economic efficiency of the processes;
- is "optimal" in the sense of maximum simplicity together with the whole functionality;
- is prepared for the later optimization, implementation and installation of the system of processes which respect the characteristics described above.

At the heart of the methodology lies the **event analysis technique.**

The goal of the technique is to identify the basic business processes inside the organization.

Events are used here to identify the basic activity chains – the business processes. Therefore, event analysis is a tool for the analysis of business activities. And the analysis of business activities is the basis for the analysis of business processes because it recognizes which activities essentially work together. These activities form what we call a **conceptual process**.

> The overall activity of the organization (we see it as the system of particular processes) is the **model of the basic goals and objectives of the organization completed by the facts which influence the possibilities for achieving these goals.**

The result of such a vision of the organization's activity is the opinion that all activities inside the organization, and their relationships, must work solely to support the organization's goals, respecting the influencing facts.

This thesis is the basic presumption for following three (mutually dependent) general principles of the methodology:

PRINCIPLE OF MODELING

The principle of modeling had been first formulated from the data point of view: the contents and structure of database objects reflect the contents and structure of real world objects. Correctness of the data model is measured by its similarity to the real world. For such measurements, the term "similarity" must be exactly defined. Therefore the special tool – the Entity Relationship Diagram (ERD), has been developed (Chen P. P. S. (1976)). ERD describes the essential characteristics of the real world: objects and their mutual relationships. It is constructed to be able to precisely describe the objects and their relationships in the same way as we see them in the real world. At the same

time, this model describes the essential requirements for the database
– it must contain the information about the same objects and their
relationships. The form in which the particular database describes
these facts always depends on the technological and implementational
characteristics of the environment in which the database is realized.
However, the essence of the model remains the same. Because of the
need to describe the same database in its various forms (essential,
technological, implementational), the principle of different architectures has been formulated. This principle, generalized to cover the
scope of the whole system (not only its database) is discussed below.
The modeling principle proves to be general, too – some parts of the
system processes have to be regarded as the model of the real world
also. However, the main problem of the so-called structured approach
in IS development is that it is not able to recognize which systems process the form of the model of the real world and which do not. Such
recognition requires the separation of the modeling operations from
the others and organizing them into the special algorithms according
to the real world objects and their relationships. This situation is not
attainable under the "structured paradigm" without accepting the
natural unity of the modeling system processes and the data in the
database. Acceptance of the natural unity of the modeling processes
and the data entities, formulated as the main OO principle, enables us
to solve Yourdon's problems with control processes – the essential
controlling algorithms follow on from the entity life histories.

As shown above, the Modeling Principle seems to be general and
independent of existing paradigms. Each new paradigm can only specify its place in IS development but cannot eliminate, or limit it.

In the area of business processes, the principle of modeling expresses the presumption that the **objective basis** for the implementation of the organization's business processes must be constituted by
real facts existing outside, and independently of, the organization.
Also relevant are those real facts which substantially influence the ability of the organization to achieve its objectives. These facts are visible
in the form of specific (critical) values of the so-called **critical factors**.
Critical changes in the critical factors values are considered so-called
(external) **events**. Events are regarded here as only the reason for starting the process – **process trigger**[2].

---

[2]   The concept of events is very broad here – it covers even such changes of facts which
are not usually regarded as "changes of critical factors' values". For example, customer
requests, or changes in production technology parameters are also regarded here as
events.

The principle of modeling states that the system of business processes in the organization is the model of relationships between the
objectives and critical events, and the mutual relationships between
the objectives, as well as between the events. The purpose of each
business process in the organization is to ensure the proper reaction
to the particular event. The essential relationships between the organization's objectives, critical factors and events are expressed in the
form of relationships between particular processes.

The purpose of the principle of modeling is:

1. It defines the basis for the analysis (what is the essential substance to be analyzed);
2. it leads to the creation of such a system of business processes
   which:
   - **is able to react to each substantial change** requiring
     also the change in the business processes (changes of
     goals, objectives and critical factors);
   - **is optimal** – it consists exclusively of **all** those process-
     es which are necessary under the given business condi-
     tions.

PRINCIPLE OF DIFFERENT PROCESS ARCHITECTURES

The principle of the "Three Architectures" was mentioned in the
paragraph in which the "modeling principle" was discussed. These two
principles interact with each other very much. The separation of the
implementation and technology-dependent aspects of the developed
Information System from the conceptual one is the essential condition
for putting the Modeling Principle into practice. Without such separation, the developer would not be able to see (and to discuss with the
user) the model of the real world in the functional and database structure of the developed IS. Three levels of the model of the IS seem to be
essential:

- *The conceptual model* represents the clear model of the real
  world, which is not "contaminated" by the non-essential aspects given by assumed technology and the implementation
  environment of the system.

- *The technological model* is based on the conceptual model enriched by the aspects given by assumed technology. Including the technological aspects often significantly changes the original – conceptual – shape of the system. For example, 3GL technology using sequential files for the realization of the database, leads to the data structures being considerably distant from the conceptual entities and their relationships. On the other hand, relational database technology preserves, to the greatest extent, the original shape of the conceptual data model. So, the degree of the shape changes always depends on the technology used.
- *The implementational model* represents the final shape of the IS. It depends on the technology used being taken into consideration in the technological model, respecting also the implementation details given by the particular environment used. Thus, the implementational model is even more distant from the real world.

Such a model of the three different views of the same thing has some general characteristics:

- each view has its own specific logic and requires specific methods of examining it, as well as a specific language for its description, which match this logic,
- for keeping the consistency between particular views it is necessary to have some means (i.e. methods and techniques) for transferring the contents of one view to the next one.

The essential relationships between the three architectures are illustrated by the following figure:

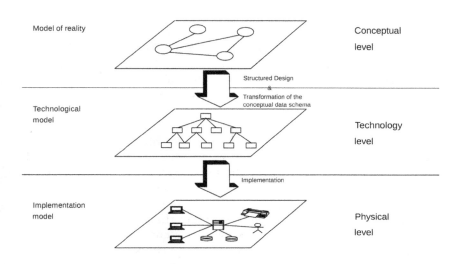

Figure 2.2. The Principle of the Three Architectures.

In the area of business processes, the principle of different architectures expresses the need to distinguish between such characteristics of the process as are given by **objective facts** (independent on the organization) – the so-called "conceptual characteristics of the process" and such characteristics which are given by the **particular context of the implementation** of the process inside the organization – the so-called "implementation characteristics of the process".

Such a model of the three different views of the same thing (system of processes) has some general characteristics:
- each view has its own specific logic and requires specific methods of examining it, as well as a specific language for its description which match this logic,
- to maintain the consistency between particular views it is necessary to have a means (i.e. methods and techniques) for transferring the contents of one view to the next one.

So each of these three levels of IS development represents a specific goal, a specific type of developer's activity, as well as the specific techniques and tools to use. Also, the transition of the design from one level to the next requires specific activities, techniques and tools.

THE PRINCIPLE OF ABSTRACTION

The Principle of Abstraction expresses the fatal need for creating abstract concepts while modeling the real world. There are more possible classifications of abstractions. Undoubtedly a very important kind of abstraction is the **Hierarchical Abstraction**.

Hierarchical abstractions are the means for **breaking down** the elements of the designed **Information System** to the level of detail. Higher-level concepts consist of the lower-level ones. On each level of detail, the elements of the developed IS and the relationships between them are described. The elements on each higher (i.e. non-elementary) level of detail are abstract concepts. Only the lowest (i.e., most detailed, elementary) level contains definite elements. There is a "tree structure" of dependencies between the concepts of the higher and lower levels, so that each element has only one parent element on the higher level (with the exception of the highest element – the root of the tree) and can have several child elements on the lower level (with the exception of the lowest elements – the leaves of the tree). Hierarchical abstractions are of two basic types:

- Aggregation. Subordinated elements are parts of the superior concept.

- Generalization. Subordinated elements are particular types of the superior concept.

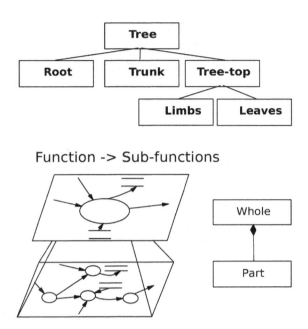

Figure 2.3. Aggregation.

Figures 2.3 and 2.4 illustrate the basic difference between both types of hierarchical abstraction. It is obvious that each of them represents a completely different meaning of relations between two concepts and thus they are mutually contradictory. However, both types occur in some form in every possible methodical viewpoint of the Information System (i.e., functional, data, or object-oriented). Therefore, each such viewpoint has to prefer one particular type of abstraction as the main view and relegate the second one to the subordinate role. David Marca (Marca, D., McGowan, C., (1992)) speaks about "constraining one abstraction type by the other".

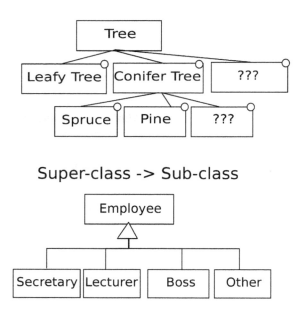

Figure 2.4. Generalization.

The aggregation type of abstraction is typically used for the breakdown processes – functions into sub-functions (using Top-Down procedure) while the generalization type of abstraction is typically used for breaking down the essential objects (classes) into sub-objects (specialization into object types)[3].

In the area of business processes, the principle of abstraction expresses the way in which particular identified facts are **analyzed in detail using hierarchical abstractions**.

There are two types of hierarchical abstractions used in the methodology:

- whole – part (aggregation),
- supertype – subtype (generalization).

---

[3] Incompatibility of these two basic approaches to the concept breakdown forms the basis for a lot of problems and misunderstandings not only in structured methods (it has often played the role of a source of vital problems of the "structured paradigm"), but also in object-oriented methods.

A **process** consists of activities. Each activity of the process can be seen as a standalone process. The difference between the concepts "process" and "activity" is always relative to the level of abstraction used. The hierarchical relationship between the process and its activities is of the type: **whole – part**.

Processes are running through the objects of the organization. These objects are the actors and/or "victims" of the processes. Each **object** may consist of sub-objects which are inheriting, and casually modifying, its basic characteristics (i.e. basic attributes of the object and also its life cycle). The hierarchical relationship between the object and its sub-objects is of the type **supertype – subtype**.

The purpose of the principle of abstraction is to use the top-down breakdown of concepts concentrating only on the essential characteristics of the particular level of abstraction. It is the means for working with the complexity of a problem.

The above described principles form the basis for all concepts, rules and their relationships defined in the methodology (see below).

2.3   PROCESS OF ANALYSIS

To formulate the business processes in the organization, first we need:

- identified basic **activities** (tasks of possible processes),
- identified basic **events** and supposed **reactions to** these events (contextual vision of the organization),
- identified basic **objects of interest** and their life cycles (object vision of the organization).

The procedure used in the business processes analysis consists of three phases:

1. **Analysis of the elementary processes**. The result of this phase is the list of elementary business processes in the organization, their structure and their mutual relationships. The basic technique used in this phase is the Analysis of the events and reactions to them.
2. **Specification of the key processes**. The result of this phase is the list of key business processes in the organization, their structure, their mutual relationships and their key attributes.

The basic technique used in this phase is the Object analysis of the organization's products. The outputs from the preceding phase – the elementary business processes – are used here as the parts of the key processes.

3. **Specification of the supporting processes.** The result of this phase is the list of supporting business processes of the organization, their structure, their mutual relationships and their key attributes. The basic technique used in this phase is the Object analysis of the organization. Analysis of the supporting business processes is based on the outputs of preceding phases – key business processes in the organization are described in detail.

The output of the business processes analysis is the conceptual process model of the organization. We suppose that the Analysis is followed by the **Implementation of the system of business processes** where particular processes are transformed into their final shape, respecting the given implementation conditions (i.e. characteristics and technology infrastructure of the organization). The implementational model of the business processes lies in the final layer of the various architectures of the process model of the organization. So, the implementation process model is the input for the successive activities of the processes installation (i.e.: preparing the organizational and technical environment for the processes, planning and performing the operation of installing the processes into the organization). One of the activities preceding the installation of the processes should also be business reengineering (it might be necessary for eliminating conflicts with the current state of the organization).

In the following text all three phases are described in more detail.

PHASE I. ANALYSIS OF THE ELEMENTARY PROCESSES

The purpose of the analysis of the elementary processes is:
- To identify the basic elementary processes in the organization.
- Using the Event analysis, to discover the internal structure of the processes and their mutual relationships (consequences) in the context of the business plan of the organization (i.e. goals and objectives defined, ways to meet the goals, critical success factors)[4].

The output of the analysis of the elementary processes is an optimized system of elementary processes, which is the basis for the specification of key processes in the organization (see the following phase).

Step 1. Analysis of events and external reactions

Purpose	To describe the reason for the existence of the organization as a system of events, and reactions to them in the context of the business plan of the organization.
Input	• Description of the organization, its goals, critical success factors of the organization and its current state. • Reference model of the business area of the organization (industry), if possible.
Output	• List of the events and organization's reactions to them including classification of the events and relationships between events and reactions. • Improved business plan of the organization, if necessary (goals, CSFs, ways to achieve the goals).
Tools and techniques	• Definition of events. • Type classification of events.

---

[4] The context of the business plan of the organization defines what is the basic sense and purpose of the organization's existence – the following model of the events, and reactions to them, will be the model of such behavior of the organization which corresponds to its business plan (thus the business plan of the organization must be used as the basis for identification of the events and reactions to them).

Step 2. Identification of basic elementary processes

Purpose   To identify the basic elementary processes using anal-
               ysis of the relationships between the events and reac-
               tions to them.

Input   ▪ List of events from the preceding step.
               ▪ Reference model of the industry, if possible.

Output   ▪ List of the elementary processes identified and their
                 relationships to the required reactions.
               ▪ Improved list of the events and reactions to them, if
                 necessary.

Tools and   ▪ Definition of event,
techniques   ▪ Type classification of events,
               ▪ Events analysis.

Step 3. Analysis and design of elementary processes relationships

Purpose   To improve the system of basic elementary processes
               to respect their mutual relationships and time de-
               pendencies.

Input   ▪ Identified elementary processes from the preceding
                 step.
               ▪ Reference model of the industry, if possible.

Output   ▪ System of the elementary processes including the
                 attributes of their mutual relationships and rela-
                 tionships to the required reactions.
               ▪ Improved list of the events, and reactions to them,
                 and elementary processes, if necessary.

Tools and   ▪ Events analysis – rules for cross reference check of
techniques   the elementary processes.

Step 4. Detailed analysis of basic elementary processes

Purpose	To describe internal structures and attributes of basic elementary processes.
Input	▪ Identified elementary processes from the preceding step including the attributes of their mutual relationships. ▪ Descriptions of jobs and activities in the organization. ▪ Reference model of the industry, if possible.
Output	▪ Descriptions of the internal structure of the basic elementary processes (break-down to the elementary activities, decomposition to the sub-processes and their attributes, if necessary). ▪ System of the elementary processes including the attributes of their mutual relationships and relationships to the required reactions. ▪ Improved list of the events, and reactions to them, and the elementary processes, if necessary.
Tools and techniques	▪ Rules for Top-Down break-down of the process. ▪ Definition of elementary process.

Step 5. Analysis of elementary processes and ensurance of consistency

Purpose	To improve the system of elementary processes to the consistent state.
Input	▪ Identified elementary processes from the preceding step including their attributes and their internal structures. ▪ Data model of the organization, if possible. ▪ Reference model of the industry, if possible.
Output	▪ Consistent system of elementary processes.
Tools and techniques	▪ Events analysis – elementary processes consistency rules. ▪ Definition of elementary process.

PHASE 2. SPECIFICATION OF THE KEY PROCESSES

The purpose of the specification of the key processes is:
- to identify key processes in the organization using object analysis of the products of the organization,
- Using the system of elementary processes from the preceding step, to discover the internal structure of the key processes and their mutual relationships.

Output of the specification of the key processes is an optimized system of conceptual key processes in the organization which is the basis for the design of the process model of the organization (by complementing the model with the supporting processes in the succeeding phase). If possible/necessary, the model of the key processes works also as the basis for business process reengineering in the organization.

Step 1. Object analysis of products

Purpose	Perform the object analysis of the products of the organization[5] to identify the basic products and their internal structures (i.e. attributes and life cycles) including the existing relationships between the objects.
Input	• List of events, and reactions to them, from the preceding steps. ▪ Data model of the organization, if possible. ▪ Reference model of the industry, if possible.
Output	▪ Object model of the organization's products consisting of: ▪ objects (products), their attributes and life cycles, ▪ relationships between the objects, including their attributes.
Tools and techniques	▪ Object analysis method, ▪ Definition of "object", ▪ Definition of object life cycle etc.

[5] Definition of the model of the products means identification of the key products of the organization (i.e. those products which are targeted outside the organization – at its customers), its attributes, relationships and life cycles. Product life cycle will be used in the following steps as the basis for the specification of proper key processes. In this sense, the analysis used must be object-oriented (simple data analysis of products as well as function analysis of the organization's behavior are insufficient approaches here).

Step 2. Identification, analysis and design of key processes

Purpose	To identify basic key processes in the organization using: identified products and their life cycles, specified elementary processes from the preceding phase.
Input	▪ System of elementary processes from the preceding phase. ▪ Object model of the organization's products from the preceding step. ▪ Reference model of the industry, if possible.
Output	▪ Descriptions of basic key processes in the organization.
Tools and techniques	▪ Definition of the key process.

Step 3. Analysis of key processes and ensurance of consistency

Purpose	Improve the system of key processes to the consistent state.
Input	▪ Descriptions of the conceptual key processes from the preceding step. ▪ Object model of the organization's products from the first step of this phase. ▪ Reference model of the industry, if possible.
Output	▪ Consistent system of key processes.
Tools and techniques	▪ Definition of key processes. ▪ Key process consistency rules.

PHASE 3. SPECIFICATION OF THE SUPPORTING PROCESSES

The purpose of the specification of the supporting processes is:
- to identify the supporting processes in the organization using the object-oriented business analysis of the organization,
- by the use of the results of the preceding two phases – system of key processes in the organization – discover the internal structure of the processes and their mutual relationships.

Output of the specification of the supporting processes is an optimized system of conceptual processes which is the basis for the design of the process model of the organization and for the implementation of this model.

Step 1. Analysis of relevant objects (object analysis of the organization)

Purpose	Perform the object analysis of the organization to identify the basic objects of interest and their internal structures (i.e. attributes and life cycles) including existing relationships between the objects.
Input	▪ Data model of the organization, if possible. ▪ Reference model of the industry, if possible.
Output	▪ Object business model of the organization consisting of: ▪ objects, their attributes and life cycles, ▪ relationships between the objects, including their attributes.
Tools and techniques	▪ Object analysis method. ▪ Definition of the business object. ▪ Definition of the object life cycle, etc.

Step 2. Identification, analysis and design of supporting processes

Purpose	To identify the supporting processes in the organization using: identified business objects and their life cycles, specified key processes from the preceding phase.
Input	<ul><li>System of processes from the preceding phase,</li><li>object model of the organization from the preceding step,</li><li>reference model of the industry, if possible.</li></ul>
Output	<ul><li>Descriptions of conceptual supporting processes in the organization.</li></ul>
Tools and techniques	<ul><li>Definition of the supporting process.</li></ul>

Step 3. Analysis of the system and consistency ensuring

Purpose	Improve the system to the consistent state.
Input	<ul><li>Descriptions of the conceptual processes from the preceding step.</li><li>Object model of the organization from the first step of this phase.</li><li>Reference model of the industry, if possible.</li></ul>
Output	<ul><li>Consistent process model of the organization.</li></ul>
Tools and techniques	<ul><li>Definition of the key and supporting processes.</li><li>Business processes consistency rules.</li></ul>

The following figure illustrates the process of the analysis:

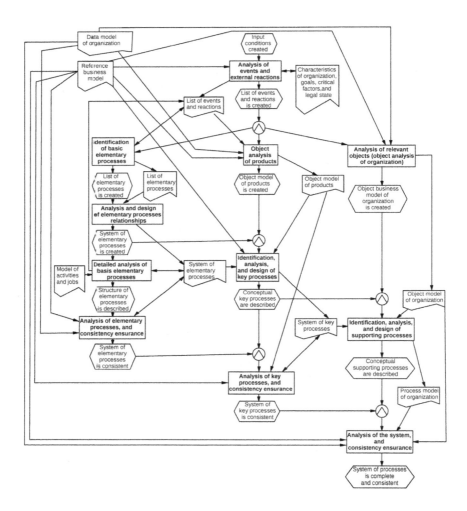

Figure 2.5. Procedure of the business processes analysis.

2.4 PROCESS MODEL AND PROCESS DIAGRAM

A significant aspect of real world behavior, seen from the process point of view – which is not present in the object point of view –is that there must be a superior reason for real world behavior, independent of the object life rules. In practice, it means that for each business process, some reason, in the form of the goal, objective, and/or external input event (customer requirement) must exist. The business process, as the collection of the actions, ordered by time and influencing the objects (their internal states and their mutual behavior), is something more than just a random collection of actions.

Similarly to the structural modeling of the real world (Object Model), even for the behavioral model (Process Model), it is necessary to describe the principles and general rules, and develop the tool (diagrammatic technique) which reflects them. The **Process Diagram**, presented in the following text, has been developed at the Department of Information Technology of the Prague University of Economics on the basis (and as a part) of the Methodology for Analyzing Business Processes (see Repa V. (1998) and Repa V. (1999a)).

The methodology is focused on creating the model of the system of business processes which:

- respects the basic objectives and goals, current state and specific characteristics of the organization;
- respects the objective circumstances (those which arise outside the organization and are independent of the organization) which can play a significant role in the behavior of the organization;
- is „optimal" in the sense of the economic efficiency of the processes;
- is „optimal" in the sense of the maximum simplicity, together with total functionality;
- is prepared for later optimization, implementation and installation of the system of processes which respect the characteristics described above.

The Process Diagram is also influenced by some ideas from Information Analysis (see Lundeberg M., Goldkuhl G., Nilsson A. (1981) and Turner, W. S., Langerhorst, R. P., Hice G. F., Eilers, H. B., Uijtenbroek, A. A. (1987)).

In light of the inconsistency with the common meaning of the term *"conceptual"* (see above the chapter Object Model And The Unified Modeling Language); for the purpose of modeling the real world processes, we use the term **Conceptual Business Processes Model**[6]. The Conceptual Business Processes Model models such processes as are necessary for achieving the business goals of the organization, and thus, are to be implemented as the workflow and supported by the Information System (IS). Such business processes are not influenced by the information technology aspects, and work as a common basis for IS development, together with workflow implementation and business processes reengineering.

The purpose of the Process Diagram as a main tool for business process modeling is to express the basic general regularity and rules of the real world in terms of a business process. The technique has to be independent of concrete conditions of the process' implementation (business technology, organization etc.) as well as conditions of the process instance and supporting information technology (workflow definition, database workflow support).

With respect to the characteristics described above, the objective of the Process Diagram is to offer a set of concepts, symbols and rules, which, if used by the modeler, is able to describe all substantial characteristics of real world behavior in as simple a way as possible.

The Business Process Metamodel (see the chapter Business Systems Modeling or Repa (2000b) for detail) describes the essential concepts of the Process Diagram together with their mutual relationships. At the center of interest, there are two main concepts:

- stimulus, and
- activity

Stimuli are of two main types:

- external (Event), and
- internal (State)

Activities are of two main types, too:

- *Processing Activity*: The purpose of this activity is to process inputs in order to obtain outputs, and
- *Control Activity:* (Decision or Logical Connector). The purpose of this activity is to ensure proper control over the process – a

---

[6]   As it is discussed also in the following chapter, the common understanding of the term *"conceptual"* tends to the synonym for "static". Thus, the concept *"conceptual model"* is usually understood as a *"model of basic terms"* which is naturally static. In the Conceptual Business Processes Model we use the term *"conceptual"* in a slightly different meaning of this word – as a *"model of the substantial elements of the business process"*, i.e., in the sense of *"the process model of the real world"*. In that sense, our use of the term *"conceptual"* is consistent with the static point of view (because from the static point of view the *"model of the real world"* is the *"model of basic terms"* as well).

succession of the correct activities according to the internal process state(s), and/or external stimuli and information.

- *Logical Connector:* is a special kind of a Control Activity defined for the simplification of the model. It is the simplest (primitive) decision, which does not need any information at the input (conjunction and disjunction).

The Processing Activity can be either Primitive (i.e., non-degradeable), or Complex. The Complex Activity can be broken-down into sub-process (i.e. a set of activities in the form of separate process models), unlike the Control Activity, which is, in principle, non-degradeable.

A description of the process **expresses the way by which the inputs are transformed into the outputs by activities in their defined succession**. Input/Output Sets are of three types:

- Information Set
- Material Set
- Mixed Set

The main purpose of such an approach is *to distinguish the **object of the processing ("material")** from the **information for the processing control** ("information")*[7]. Therefore, the term "material" is defined in a very abstract manner, here. In some specific cases (when describing the business processes of a consulting company for example), the real substance of what is called "material" here can be the information (because the "raw material", as well as the product of such a company, is the information). Even in such a situation, the need to distinguish between the subject of the processing and the control of the process remains very important.

In addition, the technique allows us to model the three external aspects of the process that we regard as the most important ones (as it follows from the purpose and principles of the methodology):

- Actors (attendees or "victims" of the process activities)
- Organization units, and
- Problems related to the process

---

[7] This part of the technique, namely, is influenced by the ISAC Method (see Lundeberg M., Goldkuhl G., Nilsson A. (1981)), particularly by its idea of distinguishing between the data as a subject of processing and the data as control information for processing. We regard the monitoring of this difference as a critical success condition for the successive development of the Information System using the business process-oriented analysis.

CRUCIAL ROLE OF PROCESS STIMULI AND ACTIVITIES

Events, states and activities of the process play a crucial role in the process model. They serve as a "meeting point" of the two main points of view existing in real world modeling:

- object model (static – structural model of the real world)
- process model (dynamic – behavioral model of the real world)

Therefore, we regard stimuli and activities as very important aspects of the process. They enable both interconnection between the object and process models, and the expression of the appropriate integrity rules.

In the process model, *states of the process* (processes) are described. A state represents a particular point within the process – the place between two particular activities. From the point of view of the first activity, the state is a *result of the activity*. From the point of view of the second one, the state is a *stimulus for the activity*.

In the object model, *states of the objects* are described. The state represents a particular point of the object life cycle – a place between two particular actions of the object. From the point of view of the first object action, the state is a *result of the action*. From the point of view of the second one, the state is a *starting point for it*.

It is obvious that the states of the process should somehow match the states of the relevant objects (i.e. those objects which are related to the process). In addition, the activities of the process, which cause some effect outside the process (i.e., Processing Activities), should also match the actions of the relevant objects. And, lastly, there is no doubt that the real world events that work as stimuli for the process activities should also, somehow, affect the relevant objects (as triggers of the object's actions).

The following two tables outline the basic requirements for the consistency rules following from the existence of these two main points of view.

The first table focuses on the external facts that have a different meaning in each of the viewpoints. The second table focuses on concepts existing in both viewpoints and having a specific meaning in each of them.

Tab. 2.1 Outline of the consistency rules requirements concerning external facts (different meanings of the same fact).

Fact	Object Model	Business Process Model
Event	Stimulus for: object internal state change, • possible communication with other objects (send the message) in the case of the "common action".	Stimulus for: • operation execution, • process state change, • output production, • possible communication with other processes (process co-ordination).
Output	Consequence of • object action, • object internal state change.	Consequence of: • operation execution (product), • process state change.

Tab. 2.2 Outline of the consistency rules requirements concerning internal concepts (different meanings of the same concept)

Concept	Object Model	Business Process Model
Action	Action executed/allowed by the object Causes: • object state change, • possible output production, • possible communication with other objects (send the message) in the case of the "common action".	Activity inside the process Causes: • process state change, • possible output production, • possible communication with other processes (co-ordination of processes).
State	Object life cycle state • starting point for action processing, • result of action processing.	Process course state • starting point for operation execution, • result of operation execution.

In the following text, the facts described in both tables are used for the formulation of basic consistency rules, addressing the relationships between the object and process models (see chapter "Modeling The Real World Under The Object Paradigm").

Process Memory

In controlling complex processes (which often have complex relationships to other processes) there is a need to store the information about the actual process state. It is a vital and conceptual condition of each process control – in the computer model of the process (i.e. conceptual need of Data Stores) as well as in the real world process implementation (the need for traditional paper evidence, for example).

Such a need occurs even in object-oriented analysis and design methodologies. For example, Jackson, M. A. (1982) offers an excellent understanding of this fact. In some object-oriented methodologies, this principle is called "the object memory" (Rumbaugh J., Blaha M., Premerlani W., Eddy F., Lorensen W. (1991), Coad P., Yourdon E. (1990)).

Using the analogy to the OO modeling methodology, we call this principle "the process memory". In the concept of "process memory", we include not only the attributes of the actual state of the process, but the data gathered by the activities, as well. Once the data are gathered, they exist inside the process and can be used by its activities without limitation (global data access). This rule also significantly reduces the complexity of the process description.

The need to store the information about the process current state serves also as the criterion for distinguishing between primitive and complex processes. When there is no need to store the information about the state of the process, the process is so simple that it is possible to take it (and implement it, as well) as a simple algorithm. The need to store the information about the state of the process always indicates the possible parallelism inside the process or at least in the communication with other processes.

For an example of a primitive process, see Figure 2.6.

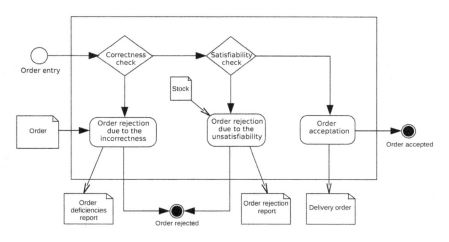

Figure 2.6. Example of a primitive process (Order Receiving).

For an example of a complex process, see Figure 2.7. In this example, the simple process *"Order Receiving"* from Figure 2.6 occurs as a single activity. It is obvious that there is a need to store the information about the state of the process between each two succeeding activities. The state *"Order accepted"* describes the need to wait for the goods' dispatching, and the state *"Goods Delivered"*, describes the need to wait for customer payment. Both situations indicate possible communication with other processes.

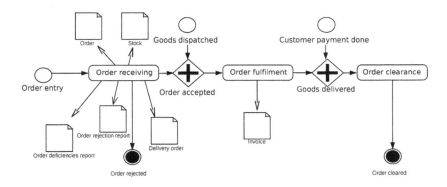

Figure 2.7. Example of a complex process.

3. Coherency of the Behavioral and Structural Models

This chapter is about the principal relationships among basic types of the real world model. Each type of model can be placed in one of the two basic categories: behavioral, and structural. Consequently, the problem of mutual coherency of models covers both fundamental aspects of the real world: structure as well as behavior. Unlike in the relatively older area of structural modeling, in the area of behavioral modeling there is still lack of mature methodology as well as a number of misunderstandings even about the basic principles. Therefore, in this chapter the initial attention is paid to the problem of modeling the dynamics.

The chapter outlines the sense, and the methodical way, of describing two basic types of the Real World processes: business processes and object life cycles. In more detail, the chapter analyzes the basic kinds of model coherency, introducing the two main criteria of completeness and correctness of models, together with the concept of the structural coherency of models.

It also discusses possible ways of describing the dynamic aspects of the real world and outlines some general conclusions.

As it is described in detail above, in the chapter 1.2, there are several approaches to conceptual modeling in the area of object-oriented methods. Each of them reduces the Object Model (represented by the Class Diagram) to the model of objects and the relationships between them, represented by their attributes, but not by their methods. This reduction is present also in Roni Weisman's approach (Weisman, R. (1999)), even though he considers, in addition to "Entities", also "Control Objects". Just the fact of distinguishing between "static" and "dynamics assuring" objects is the best demonstration of such a reduction. The common understanding of the term "conceptual", thus, tends to be a synonym for "static".

However, such an approach contrasts with the basic principle, and the main contribution, of the object-oriented paradigm – **unity of data and operations**. This principle evokes the idea that **it is necessary to model not only the static aspects of the Real World, but also its dynamics**. The existence of the object as the collection of data (attributes) and functions (methods) is to be the correct reason for data processing operations control – strictly speaking: the **object life cycle**.

Figure 3.8 illustrates the object life cycle as a complement to the Class Diagram. It can be seen that all methods of the conceptual object should be ordered into one algorithm which describes the place of each method in the overall process of the object's life. This placement of the method defines the conceptual meaning of it.

3.1 TYPES OF PROCESSES IN THE REAL WORLD

The last paragraph argues for recognizing the dynamics inside the conceptual model. The problem of dynamics in the Real World Model is, usually, closely connected with the phenomenon of the business processes. Hence, the model of the business processes is usually regarded as the only significant description of the real world dynamics. Consequently, the conceptual model is usually regarded as being a clearly static description of the real world. Another extreme opinion considers the Class Diagram as the appropriate tool for business process description and reduces the natural need for the description of the process dynamics just on the description of the business processes global attributes, and relationships among them (the standard UML profile for BP modeling, for example).

Experience shows that the above stated opinions inadmissibly reduce the substance of the problem of the Real World dynamics and, in the end, lead to incorrect conclusions.

Figure 3.1 describes the two main dimensions of the Real World Model:
- the *structure* of the real world (the view of the real world as a set of objects and their relationships),
- the *behavior* of the real world (the view on the real world as a set mutually connected business processes).

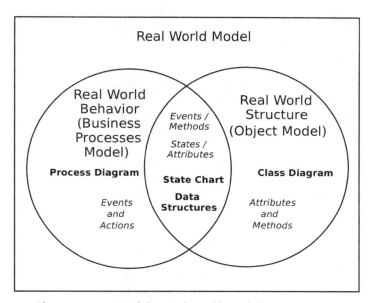

Figure 3.1. Two Dimensions of the Real World Model.

On the figure it is clearly visible that the concept of "behavior" cannot be regarded as a synonym for the "dynamics". Both dimensions have a common intersection. Even inside the Real World Structure it is thus necessary to consider some dynamics – the intersection contains, besides the static object, aspects such as attributes and data structures, as well as typical dynamic aspects like events, methods, and object states. Thus the description of dynamics is not just a matter of the behavioral model. It concerns the conceptual model, as well.

Obviously there are two types of dynamics in the real world:
- dynamics of the real world objects, represented by their life cycles,
- behavior in the real world, represented by business processes.

Some arguments in favour of the above stated ideas:

The real world objects cannot be regarded as business processes because:
- objects do not behave in any way – their life cycles are, rather, the description of business rules in a process manner;
- the process of the object life has no goal (except the "death" of the object), nor product; it is rather the expression of the objective necessity;

- although we describe the process of the objects life-cycles, that description still remains the structural one – the whole context is described statically (structurally), it is subordinated to the structure of the Real World;
- objects are typically take on different roles in different processes giving them the context (Real World Rules).

From the opposite viewpoint, the business process is quite a different kind of process than the life-cycle of the object, because:

- the business process has a goal, and a product, it is a typical expression of the human will;
- the business process usually combines different objects giving them a specific meaning (roles of actors, products, etc.).

For a detailed discussion of the main differences between object life cycles and business processes see Repa, V. (1996), Repa, V. (1999a), Repa, V. (1999b), Repa V. (2000a), and Repa, V. (2003).

The above mentioned facts support the need for modeling the dynamics of the conceptual objects as something different from the behavior of the real world, which is traditionally represented by the business processes. Although in both cases we consider the modeling of processes, at the same time we have to take into account the fact that modeling of the conceptual objects' dynamics has its own specific logic, different from the logic of the modeling of business processes. This logic primarily reflects the specific nature of the object life cycles, as discussed above.

3.2 MODELING OBJECT LIFE CYCLES

For the purpose of describing the object life cycles, the most suitable tool from the Unified Modeling Language (UML) is the State Chart.

The State Chart is not primarily intended for the description of the life cycle; its roots are in the area of the State Machines Theory, and it is closely connected with the concept of the so called "real-time processing". However, the concept of the state machine in general is not substantially reducible just to the area of real-time processing. Also, in the area of data processing, there is the need for recognizing states and transitions among them. The best proof of this idea is the concept of the object life cycle itself – once we think about the objects generally (i.e. in terms of their classes), then we must sharply distinguish between the class and its instance. In the case of the object life, this is necessary to determine those points in the life of all objects of the same class, which we will be able to identify, and which it is necessary to identify in order to describe the synchronization of the object life with the life cycles of other objects. Such points of the object life are its states. So, each object instance lives its own life while the lives of all instances of the same class are described by the common life cycle.

As can be seen on Figure 3.8, the State Chart describes the possible (allowed) states of the object together with the possible transitions among them. Each transition is described with two attributes:

- reason for the transition (upper part of the transition description),
- method of the transition realization (lower part of the transition description).

Each described life cycle has to correspond to the particular object class in the Class Diagram. In such a way, the State Chart specifies the general mechanism of the life of all possible instances of the given class. The described states and transitions among them consequently correspond to the attributes and methods of the class. The life cycle states represent, in fact, the specific attribute of the class (this attribute is not present in the class description but it exists by the definition – it is necessary to distinguish among the particular states/values of this "hidden" attribute). Each transition between life cycle states then represents the use of the particular class method.

While the method of transition realization corresponds to the specific **method of the given class**, the reason for the transition corresponds to the specific **event (external influence)** which causes the transition.

The concept of events, as a common concept existing in both main points of view of the real world dynamics, allows **linking** of the description of **object life cycles with** the description of the **business processes** (see below).

3.3 MODELING BUSINESS PROCESSES

The Process Diagram Technique aims to offer a set of concepts, symbols and rules, using which the modeler is able to describe all substantial characteristics of real world behavior in as simple a way as possible.

On the web page of the OpenSoul project (OpenSoul (2000)), one can find the process meta-model which describes the key concepts of the technique together with their relationships.

The process model contains the crucial role play events, states and activities of the process. They serve as a "meeting point" of the two main points of view existing in real world modeling:
- object model (static–structural model of the real world),
- process model (dynamic–behavioral model of the real world).

Therefore, we consider the stimuli and activities as very important aspects of the process. They enable the interconnection between the object and process models as well as enabling the expression of the appropriate integrity rules.

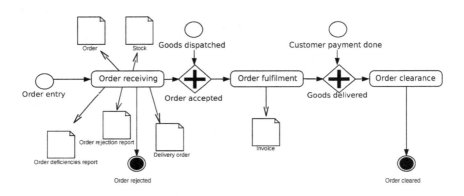

Figure 3.2. Example of the Business Process Model (BPMN notation).

Figure 3.2 illustrates the use of the above stated technique. It shows how the process description emphasizes the most important aspects of the process:
- events and their consequences – process activities and states (i.e. points of waiting for the event) on the one hand,
- inputs and outputs processed by the process, including the main process product (i.e. the main reason for the process run), on the other hand.

3.4 Coherency of models

Regarding the coherency of models, let us introduce two basic criteria:
- *completeness* of models,
- *correctness* of models.

As Figure 3.3 illustrates, completeness and correctness are mutually interconnected. On the level of the particular diagrams, each criterion has a specific meaning. But in the intersections of particular diagrams, and, even more so, in the intersections of all three diagrams, both criteria come together. More precisely: the correctness of the models has the form of completeness of the superior general concepts (relations, roles, actions, and reasons) in them.

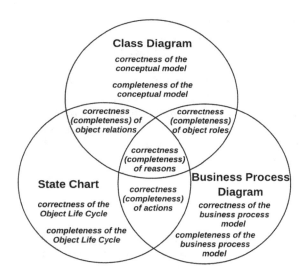

Figure 3.3. Criteria of Completeness and Correctness in Diagrams.

The specific kind of models coherency is the coherency of the main types of structures, which occur in all viewpoints in several forms. I call this kind of model coherency *structural coherency*. It is described in the following chapter.

COMPLETENESS

Completeness has the specific form in each model (diagram):

Completeness of the conceptual model generally follows from the theory of conceptual modeling, where the basic rules for this criterion are defined. For instance, one of the main rules is: "There must be at least one way between any two classes in the Class Diagram."

Completeness of the business process model generally follows from the theory of business processes reengineering and modeling, where the content of this concept in the field of business processes is defined. For instance, some of the main rules are: "There must be a business process model described for each specified product.", or, "Each recognized event must be used in at least one business process model as a reason for some action." (By the way: this rule defines the objective need for the breaking down of the processes – we need to break-down the processes until we place all the events).

Completeness of the Object Life Cycles is expressed by the simple rule "The Object Life Cycle must cover the whole life of the object." As a realization of this rule, the methodology defines three mandatory types of object methods (stereotypes): constructor, destructor, and transformer. The purpose is to ensure the completeness of the whole object life in the description.

CORRECTNESS

Correctness of the conceptual model is defined as follows: "Each object class must correspond to the real and existing objects. Any relationship to other object class(es) must model the existing possible relationship. The described object classes and their relationships must be valid for all possible instances of each object class."

Correctness of the business process model is defined as follows: "The business process must fulfill the main process goal. Described process actions, their succession, inputs, outputs and other attributes must be valid for all possible instances of the process."

Correctness of Object Life Cycles is defined as follows: "The Object Life Cycle must correspond to the real and objective actions and their successions in the life of the object. The Object Life Cycle must be valid for all possible instances of the object class."

CORRECTNESS AND COMPLETENESS

Correctness (completeness) of object relations considers the relationships between State Chart and Class Diagram and it is defined as follows: "Each association belonging to the class in the Class Diagram must correspond to some method specified in the object life cycle (State Chart) of this class as an attribute of the state transition, and vice versa."

Correctness (completeness) of object roles considers the relationships between the Class Diagram and the Business Process Diagram and it is defined as follows: "Each object class must be present in some Business Process as an Input, or Output Set, Actor or any other external factor, and vice versa."

Correctness (completeness) of actions considers the relationships between the Business Process Diagram and the State Chart and it is defined as follows: "Each action in each business process must correspond to at least one transition between states in at least one object life cycle, and vice versa."

Correctness (completeness) of reasons considers the relationships among all three diagrams and it is defined as follows: "Each event used in each Object Life Cycle as a reason for the state transition should correspond to the same event used in at least one Business Process as a reason for the process activity, and vice versa."

3.5 STRUCTURAL COHERENCY

The roots of the idea of structural coherency are in ideas of Michael Jackson, formulated in his method "JSP" (Jackson, M. A. (2002)).

According to the author, the fundamental idea of JSP was: the *program structure should be dictated by the structure of its input and output data streams* (Jackson, M. A. (1975)). If one of the sequential files processed by the program consisted of customer groups, each group consisting of a customer record followed by some number of order records, each of which is either, a simple order or an urgent order, then the program should have the same structure: it should have a program part that processes the file, with a subpart to process each customer group; and that subpart should itself have one subpart that processes the customer record, and so on.

The execution sequence of the parts should mirror the sequence of records and record groups in the file. The program parts could be very small and not, in general, separately compiled.

The resulting structure can be represented in a JSP structure diagram, as in Figure 3.4:

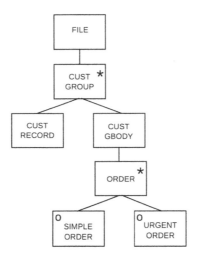

Figure 3.4. Structure of a File and of a Program (Jackson, M. A. (2002)).

The structure is simultaneously the structure of the file and the structure of a program to process the file. As a data structure it may be verbalised like this:

"The File consists of zero or more Customer Groups. Each Customer Group consists of a Customer Record followed by a Customer Group Body. Each Customer Group Body consists of zero or more Orders. Each Order is either a Simple Order or an Urgent Order." (Jackson, M. A. (2002)).

Based on the above stated idea Jackson proposed the process of designing the program which consists of the following steps:

1. Draw data structures for program input(s) and output(s).
2. Form the program structure based on the data structures from the previous step.
3. List and allocate operations to the program structure.
4. Create the elaborated program structure with operations and conditions added to the basic program structure.
5. Translate the structure diagram into the structure text or program code.

The result of applying JSP is a program that reflects the problem structure as expressed in a model of its inputs and outputs (see Figure 3.5). If changes to the program are required that only affect local components, the changes can be easily made to the corresponding program components. A program's structural integrity – its correspondence with the problem's structure – is the main way we can reduce errors and costs in software maintenance.

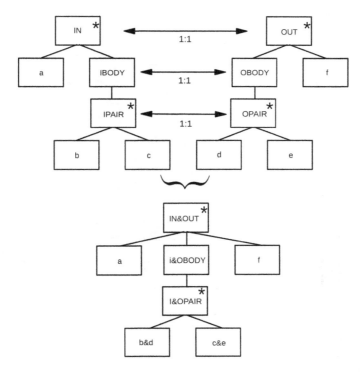

Figure 3.5. Two File Structures and a Program Structure (Jackson (2002)).

The crucial moment of the design process is the first step and the transition from the first to the second step. In fact, *the root of the problem is solved by merging data structures together* – it requires making a set of crucial decisions about the correspondences of the particular data structures' parts and their merging into the resulting structure (which is, in fact, the structure of the transformation process from the input structure(s) to the output one(s)). Therefore, Jackson determined the set of rules for merging structures together. In addition to this set of rules, he defined the concept of the "structure clash":

If there are two not corresponding components of the corresponding iterations, and if it is not possible to merge them as a sequence, or as a selection, nor to express the first component as an iteration of the second one (and vice versa,) then, there is the structure clash existing between both structures. (see Figure 3.6).

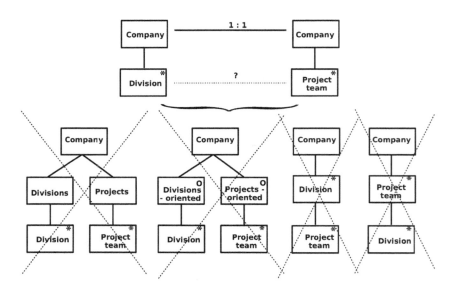

Figure 3.6. Structure clash.

The structure clash means that it is *impossible* to express the substance of the problem as a *simple structure*. The process of solving the problem, consequently, requires several *parallel* solution processes, each targeted on separate, and relatively independent, parts of the whole problem (sub-problem). For instance, in the example given in Figure 3.6, the solution (i.e. transformation of the company from the division-oriented organization to the project-oriented one), requires breaking the company organization up first of all, and then building the new organization which is harmonized with the project management requirements. This is because the division organizations, and the project organization, are mutually independent in so far as it is not possible to make any compromise, or to subordinate one structure to the second one.

Thus the *structure clash* (from Jackson's theory) is the precise technical *definition of natural parallelism* in the process, stemming from the nature of the problem itself and, therefore, substantially present.

Unfortunately, the Structure Diagram, used in previous paragraphs, is not a regular diagram of the UML. While using the UML it is necessary to use the State Chart for a description of the object life cycles.

The State Chart is not primarily intended for a description of the life cycle; its roots are in the area of the State Machines Theory, and it is closely connected with the concept of the so called "real-time processing". But the concept of the state machine, in general, is not substantially reducible just to the area of real-time processing. Also, in the area of data processing there is a need for recognizing states and transitions among them. The best proof of this idea is the concept of the object life cycle itself – once we think about the objects generally (i.e., in terms of their classes), then we have to strongly distinguish between the class and its instance. In the case of the object life this requires us to determine those points in the life of all objects of the same class, which we will be able to identify, and which it is necessary to identify in order to describe the synchronization of the object life with life cycles of other objects. Such aspects of the object life are its states. So each object instance lives its own life while the lives of all instances of the same class are described by the common life cycle.

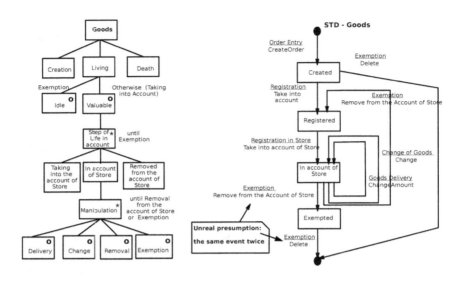

Figure 3.7. Structure Diagram versus State Chart.

It can be seen that the difference between these two styles of describing exactly reflects the basic difference between the structured and unstructured point of view. In the structured view there is the need for creating abstract, higher units (such as "Living" and "Filling"), which serves as the means of understanding the problem. Such a possibility is missing in the case of the State Chart. On the other hand, the State Chart allows for the opposite point of view of the object life cycle – in terms of states and transitions between them. Such a view is very close to the position of a real attendee of the business (i.e., real world behavior), who typically sees the process in detail. One very serious problem is that unstructured description often leads to the creation of subsidiary abstract concepts which have nothing to do with the real world (i.e. concepts which are not "conceptual"). In our example there is the problem with the presumption that the same event "Exemption" occurs twice, which is impossible in the real world. The reason for this is the impossibility of expressing the necessary combination of actions connected to this event in the given situation (object state).

At the end of this chapter let us recapitulate some of the limitations of the state-oriented description:

- An unstructured view of the process requires the need for the additional reader's abstraction in order to recognize the structures.
- For a description of the generalized processes it is necessary to use the hierarchy of diagrams (compound states). When we describe the life-cycle of the object class, this necessity is warranted because such a process is generalized by definition.

On the other hand, the main limitation of the operation-oriented description is the fundamental need for the reader's abstraction – the reader needs to generalize sets of operations in order to recognize the basic structure types (iteration, sequence, and selection). This need is missing in the state-oriented view of the life-cycle, where the description strictly follows particular state transitions. Nevertheless, this abstraction is necessary for recognizing deeper – structural – consequences of models.

3.6 MUTUAL CONSISTENCY OF OBJECTS' LIFE CYCLES

Jackson's rules for merging structures, as described above, allow us to take the structure as a common denominator of both the data and the process and use of this structure as the basis for mapping deeper conjunctions among data structures and processes.

Moreover, there are some other general analogies which could be useful for utilising Jackson's ideas for reflecting the natural consequences in Real World Models, which follow on from the nature of the relationships among the Real World Objects. In the following text I call them *structural consequences*.

The main, and the most important, general analogies, mentioned above, are:

- The *sequence* type of structure is an analogy to the *aggregation* type of hierarchy, while the *selection* type of structure is an analogy to the *generalization* type of hierarchy. In this connection, it is necessary to take into consideration that the *iteration* type of structure is just a special case of the sequence (where all its parts are of the same structure), hence it is an analogy to the *aggregation*.

- The *cardinality* of the relationships among objects is an analogy to the *aggregation* (as the aggregation reflects the quantity and says nothing about the quality), whilst the *optionality* of the relationship is an analogy to the *generalization* (as the generalization reflects the quality and says nothing about the quantity (including the ordering)).
- Similarly, the generalization (inheritance) type of relationship in the class diagram should be reflected by some kind of selection, whilst the aggregation (composition) should be reflected by some kind of sequence/iteration, with all consequences following from it.

Jackson's theory does not only describe the rules for merging structures together. It also leads to the important idea that structural coherency is the crucial point for modeling the basic relationships between the static dimension of the real world (what it consists of), and its dynamic dimension (how it is doing). Each point of view of the real world, including the conceptual model, has these two dimensions. In the conceptual model of the real world the static dimension is modeled by the conceptual object classes and their relationships, whilst the dynamics of them is modeled by their life cycles.

We may conclude from previous paragraphs that we can formalize basic rules for the structural consistency of objects in the conceptual model as follows:

- Each association between two object classes must be reflected by a specific operation in each class life cycle.
- The cardinality of the association must be reflected by a corresponding type of structure in the life cycle of the opposite class: cardinality 1:n by the iteration of parts, cardinality 1:n by the single part of the structure.
- The optionality of the association must be reflected by a corresponding selection structure in the life cycle of the opposite class.
- Each generalization of the class must be reflected by a corresponding selection structure in its life cycle.
- Each aggregation association between classes must be reflected by a corresponding iteration structure in the life cycle of the aggregating class (container/composite class).

Figure 3.8 illustrates some examples of structural coherences in the conceptual model. The Class Diagram represents the static contextual view of reality, while the object life cycle describes the "internal dynamics" of the class. The internal dynamics of the class should be subordinated to the context (i.e. substantial relationships to the other classes); therefore, each class contains a specific operation (method) for each association (it is obvious that some associations to other classes are missing in this example). The life cycle determines the placement of each particular operation in the overall life history of the object – the internal context of the operation. The internal context must be consistent with the external one, which follows from the relationships described between classes in the Class Diagram (associations to other classes, generalizations etc.). Dashed arrows indicate the basic consequences of the described associations and their cardinalities in the life cycles of both classes:

- Optionality of the association (goods may not to be ordered at all) is reflected by the existence of the possibility that the whole sub-structure, representing the ordering of goods may be idle in the Goods life cycle. Also, the fundamental conditionality of the delivery is a reflection of this fact.

- Multiplicity of the association (one Order may contain several items) is reflected by the iteration of the structure "Filling" in the Order life history, which expresses the fundamental fact that the order may be created, fulfilled by several supplies, or changed several times; separately for each ordered item.

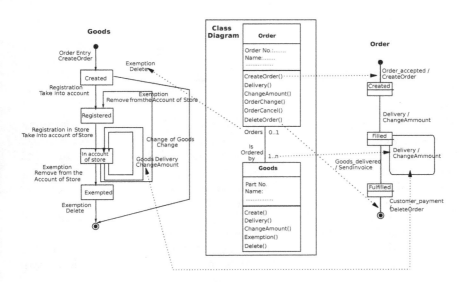

Figure 3.8. Structural Coherency of Objects and their Life Cycles.

Knowledge of the structural consequences helps the analyst to improve the Real World Models concerning their mutual consistency, as well as, their relative completeness (as completeness is a main part of the issue of consistency).

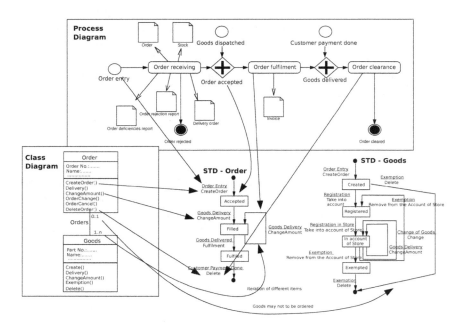

Figure 3.9. Example of the coherency of models.

Figure 3.9 illustrates how the process model explains the dependencies between objects and their life cycles, giving them a superior sense. This explanation is based on the perception of object actions in terms of reasons for them – events and process states. Objects are playing the roles of attendees, or victims (subjects), of the processes. For completeness it is necessary to regard the fact that one object typically occurs in more processes, as well as in one process. It typically combines the attendance of more objects. The orthogonality of those two points of view is also typical and substantial – it gives sense to this coupling. Structure and behavior is the analogy of two basic dimensions of the real world – space and time.

Even the specified consistency rules work together in mutual coherency. This means that there should be considered a number of additional second- and third-level consistency rules following on from the combination of basic rules. For example: We suppose that each event specified in the Object Life Cycles is used in some Business Process(es); (the rule for correctness (completeness) of reasons); and, at the same time we require each state transition in the object life cycle to correspond to some association with another object class (the rule for correctness (completeness) of object relations). From this combination of rules it follows that we suppose that each event causes some business action (as it is defined in the business process model), and that it causes the state transition of some object (as it is defined in the object life cycle), and that it creates the link to some other object at the same time. In fact, this means that each business process activity has logical consequences in the mutual behavior of objects (and vice versa[8]).

3.7 POSSIBLE WAYS OF DESCRIBING THE DYNAMICS OF THE REAL WORLD

To conclude from the previous chapters, we can see that there are two main approaches to the description of the dynamics of the Real World:

Business Process Approach is characterized with the modeling Business Processes on the one hand, and, the Object Life Cycles on the other, thus taking care of their mutual consistency. In this approach, the Object Life Cycles are playing the role of the process-manner description of "Business Rules" – a process description of crucial restrictions given by business which are naturally static (in spite of the fact that they are described as processes (of object lives)).

The advantage of this approach:

Two basic viewpoints of the modeled Real World (the intentional one – business process – versus the static one – object life cycles) allow the dramatic refinement of the set of rules defining the correctness (completeness) of the models.

---

[8]   In fact, here we deal with the famous "chicken-and-egg dilemma"; deciding whether the mutual behavior of objects is the consequence of business process activities or whether business process activities are, rather, given by the actor's behavior. This problem is connected with the two basic ways of describing the dynamics of the Real World which are discussed below.

The disadvantage of this approach:
This approach is not open – all possible actions are described in the form of business processes, actors have no chance to function outside of these processes. It means that this approach always reduces the large-scale reality just on the subset defined by the models. This can cause serious restrictions in the ability to change traditional rules; which is still more important in our turbulent world.

The *"Legislative Approach"* is characterized with the modeling of the objects and their mutual relationships, presuming them to be real world agents with their own activity. We should also take care of the mutual consistency of objects and their life cycles. In this approach, the "Life Cycles" have the role of describing the basic "Real World" rules which have to be respected by any object's behavior. Those objects from the model which represent the "Actors" are regarded as "Real World" agents with their own activity. They behave actively and independently, respecting just the rules given them via their life cycles and mutual dependencies on other objects. Thus, there is no need to model "Business Processes" – the Class Diagram together with models of the life cycles just "delineate the space" for objects' behavior – i.e. basic "legislation". Therefore, I call this approach *the Legislative Approach*.

The advantage of this approach:
This approach is more open, and, thus, potentially closer to reality than the Business Process approach. In the real world, actors are usually acting according to the rules given by their own activity. All possible ways of acting are taken into account.

The disadvantage of this approach:
The missing presumption of intentional sets of real world actions, in the form of described business processes, reduces the possibility of formulating integrity rules which could reduce the set of possible agent actions to a set of correct ones only (in the sense of described business processes). For instance, see the rules for completeness and correctness of object roles for reasons, which are completely useless when the business process description is missing.

Figure 3.10 shows the context of both above discussed approaches. The "Legislative Approach" is suitable when the level of maturity in knowledge management is high. As it represents the vague management style, it strongly depends on the self-organizing ability of the system. On the other hand the "Business Process" approach is suitable only when the ability for the real world rules description is high – i.e., in the terms of a relatively static and well structured environment.

It seems that the correct way lies in the combination of both approaches which allows us to overcome their limitations. In particular, it means the need to, firstly, find the role of active objects in business processes. This is the main idea behind the further development of the methodology.

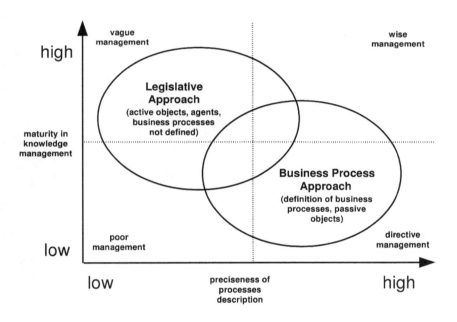

Figure 3.10. Two main approaches to the description of the dynamics of the Real World.

4. SERVICE-ORIENTED BUSINESS PROCESS MANAGEMENT

This chapter deals with the role of the concept of services in the area of Business Process Management and Reengineering. It describes the process of the Business Processes System Design which is a part of the Methodology for Business Processes Analysis and Design – MMAPB. The design technique covers the whole process from the identification of the basic activities to the design of key and supporting processes as late as the building of the resulting infrastructures. A very important tool in the structuring of the processes is the principle of services. It allows us to discover the basic supporting processes in the bodies of key processes, their clarification with the exact definition of the interfaces between processes, and, finally, the exact definition of the needs and possibilities of the supporting infrastructures.

The chapter argues in support of thinking in terms of services as being much more useful and the general principle to be limited to the area of technology and software systems development only.

4.1 BUILDING PROCESS MANAGED ORGANIZATION

The first complete explanation of the idea of process management as a style of managing an organization has already been published (Hammer M., Champy J. (1994)). The authors excellently explain the historical roots, as well as the necessity, of focusing on business processes in the management of the organization. The major reason for the process-orientation in management is the vital need for the dynamics in the organization's behavior. It has to be able to reflect all substantial changes in the market as soon as possible. The only way to link the behavior of the organization to the changes in the market is to manage the organization as a set of processes principally focused on customer needs. As customer needs are constantly changing, the processes in the organization should change as well. That means that any process in the organization should be linked to the customer's needs as directly as possible. Thus, the general classification of processes in the organization distinguishes mainly between:

- **key processes**, i.e. those processes in the organization which are linked directly to the customer, covering the whole business cycle from expression of the customer need to its satisfaction with the product/service;
- **supporting processes**, which are linked to the customer indirectly – by means of key processes which they are supporting with particular products/services.

Whilst the term "key process" typically covers whole business cycle with the customer – it is focused on the particular business case; the supporting process is typically specialized just to the particular service/product, which means that its product is more universal – usable in a number of business cases. This approach allows the organization to focus on the customers and their needs (by means of the key processes), and to use all the traditional advantages of the specialization of activities (by means of the supporting processes) at the same time. Key processes play the crucial role – by means of these processes the whole system of mutually interconnected processes is tied together with the customers' needs. Supporting processes are organized around the key ones, so that the internal behavior, specialization, and even the effectiveness of the organizations' activities are subordinated to the customers and their needs.

Once we accept the ideas of process managed organization stated above we need to answer the set of consequential questions about how to design such a system:

- "how to find the right structure of business processes which respects professional standards to be able to fully exploit possibilities of outsourcing, and, at the same time, is driven by the naturally changing as well as naturally specific key processes?"
- "how to design the organizational aspects as the system of competencies and responsibilities, working positions, organization structure, etc. which are explicit, understandable, and are working as a standard, and, at the same time, which are flexible enough to be able to fully support naturally changing processes?"

- "how to design the information system which follows, as closely as possible, the technology standards in order to fully exploit its possibilities, and, at the same time, which is flexible enough to be able to support naturally changing processes in full detail?"

The view of the behavior of a process-managed organization is quite different from the traditional one. Mainly, the key processes represent an unusual view of communication and collaboration within the organization. In traditionally managed organizations the organization structure reflects just the specialization of work; it is static, and hierarchical. The concept of key processes brings the necessary dynamics to the system – key processes often change according to the customer needs, while supporting ones are relatively stable (the nature of the work is relatively independent of the customers' needs). At the same time, the key processes represent the most specific part of the organizations' behavior, while the supporting ones are more general and standard. Thus, the supporting processes are the best candidates for possible outsourcing while the key ones should be regarded, rather, as an essence of the market value of the organization. So, we have a system of processes with very different nature. To ensure the necessary communication among them, we need to have the interface which enables us to overcome these differences.

We can also see similar problems with the interface among the system of business processes and its supporting infrastructures: organizational structure, and information system. In both cases we have to harmonize different systems working differently, with different goals, and under different circumstances (see the questions at the beginning of this sub-section).

The starting point for all infrastructures (i.e., organization structure, and information system) is always the real structure (i.e., structure of business processes in the organization). So that the right solution of the main problem – coordination and harmonization of business processes – must be the starting point for the solution of consequential problems with infrastructures. Coordinating business processes we, at the same time, create the basis for both: harmonization of substantially different interests and responsibilities of different organizational roles, as well as harmonization of substantially different business processes versus processes of the information system.

This chapter proposes the use of the **concept of Service as a common general solution of all the problems** stated above. It argues for thinking in terms of services when analyzing the interface among business processes. Firstly, we need to define the parameters of each connection point of two processes with respect to both sides of this relation – as the **service offered by the supporting process to the supported one**. This way the idea of a process managed organization perfectly fits the idea of the service-oriented structure of a system. Moreover, a system of business processes, created in such a way, is the best basis for creating naturally harmonized infrastructures as it will be shown in the following section.

4.2 DESIGNING THE SYSTEM OF BUSINESS PROCESSES

The technique presented in this chapter is a part of the Methodology for Business Process Analysis and Design (MMABP). This methodology is presented in more detail in (Repa, (2003)) and published on the web in (Repa, 2000b) and (OpenSoul (2000)). The methodology covers both substantial dimensions of a business system model. Although this chapter is focused just on the dimension of the business processes, the second dimension of the business objects also permanently influences the procedure. This influence is described in (Repa (2004)) and (Repa (2007)). Some details of the object dimension of a business system model itself can be found in (Repa (2008)), for instance.

Figure 4.1 shows three basic models which the description of the system of business processes consists of:

- **Global model of processes** which expresses the structure of the system of processes with their mutual associations: communication of key and supporting processes.
- **Models of the process run** describing the basic logic of the process run. In fact, it is the **model of the process detail**. The logic of the key processes determines the meaning of the supporting processes. It is necessary to model the process logic just for those processes which are chosen to be the subject of detailed interest (see below).
- **Basic process attributes** in the form of a table containing the basic attributes of each important process. The basic attributes should be described for each process. They represent the basic

characteristics of the process (starting event, product, goal, specific conditions, etc.). Even if it has been decided to outsource the process, it is necessary to specify its basic characteristics (as they are the basis for the SLA specification in this case).

More detailed descriptions of the global and the detail process model are following.

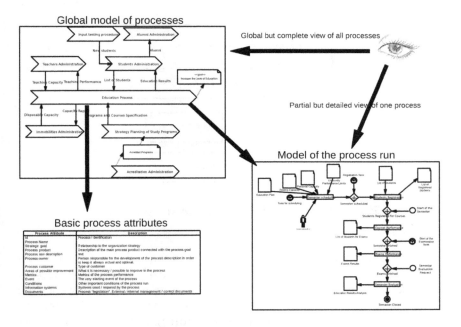

Figure 4.1. Global versus detailed model of business processes.[9]

---

[9] This figure is just an illustration of different views and diagrams. Unreadable text is not important.

GLOBAL MODEL OF PROCESSES

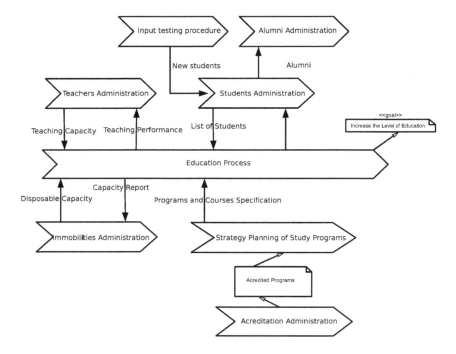

Figure 4.2. Example of the global model of business processes (Eriksson-Penker notation).

The global model of processes represents the static view of the system of business processes. It describes the existence of the processes and their mutual associations/connections. The methodology uses the Eriksson-Penker notation (Eriksson, Penker (2000)) for this model, which is an extension of the UML (UML (2010))[10]. This fact emphasizes the "static" nature of this model, by the way.

The standard process attributes (goal, product, starting event, etc.) can be described for those processes where it is important. Normally,

---

[10]   In fact, any other suitable notation, like Aris for instance, can be used in place of the BPMN and Eriksson-Penker Notation. The reason for the use of these notations is the fact that they are standardized with principal respect to the UML which is the widely respected standard used in both: analytical as well as IS Development activities. This fact we regard as very important in the MMABP methodology. Complete methodology content together with the definition of requirements for diagrammatic tools can be found in OpenSoul (2000), and Repa, V. (2000b).

all key processes together with some important supporting processes should be specified this way. If it has been decided to outsource the supporting process, it is also necessary to specify its basic attributes, for example.

The key information which this model brings is the division of all activities in the organization into the processes of two basic types:

- **Key process** is the process producing the basic product of the organization. It brings value to the customer, and profit to the organization, respectively. Key processes define the basic meaning of the organization; they justify its existence. Example of a key process is the Education process in Figure 4.2 – it represents the main value of the university for its customers.
- **Supporting process** is the process whose existence is defined by the services offered to other processes (the key or supporting ones). Basic types of supporting processes are:
  - Sub-process – the process specialized in the production of a particular service/product as a final output. An example of such process in Figure 4.2 is the Input testing procedure.
  - The horizontal supporting process with a relatively independent logic, offering the service to a number of other processes. An example of such process in Figure 4.2 is the Student Administration Process.

MODEL OF THE PROCESS RUN

As stated above, the Model of the process run represents the detailed view of a particular process. Those processes which are to be the subject of detailed analysis (i.e. key processes as well as the most important supporting processes) should be specified this way – as a structure of succeeding activities and states. MMABP methodology contains the technique (the so-called Process Diagram Technique) which was created to ensure the quality and completeness of such description. The Process Diagram Technique aims to offer a set of concepts, symbols and rules, by using which the modeler is able to describe all the substantial characteristics of the real world behavior in as simple a way as possible. The methodology uses the standard BPMN notation (BPMN (2006)) for this model.

Key concepts of the technique, together with their relationships, are the subject of the OpenSoul project (OpenSoul (2000)), which provides the process meta-model. At the centre of interest there are two main concepts:

- stimuli (external (Event) or internal (State)), and
- activities (processing or decision (or logical connectors conjunction and disjunction)).

The description of the process expresses the way the inputs are transformed into outputs by the activities in their defined succession. In addition, the technique allows modeling of the external aspects of the process (actors, organizational units, problems, and any other relevant aspect connected with the process).

For more detailed description of the basic concepts of this model and their relationships see the chapter 2.4 above, for the exact definition of them see the meta-model (Repa (2000b)).

Events, states, and activities of the process play a crucial role in the process model. They serve as a "meeting point" of the two main points of view existing in real world modeling:

- object model (static or structural model of the real world),
- process model (dynamic or behavioral model of the real world).

Therefore, we regard the stimuli and activities as important aspects of the process. They enable interconnection between the object and process models, as well as enabling the expression of the appropriate integrity rules.

At the same time, events and states are also "meeting points" of mutually collaborating processes. They represent two complementing views of the "business relation" of two processes; consumer and supplier. From the point of view of the consumer process, this "business relation" is a process state (the consumer process must wait for the service). From the point of view of the supplier process, this "business relation" is an event (call for service). Thus, such a view of the process, where its internal structure expresses the collaboration with other processes, generally makes up the idea of the **service oriented process thinking**.

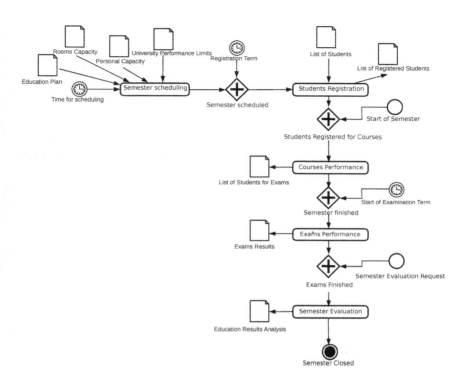

Figure 4.3. Example of the model of business process run (BPMN notation).

Figure 4.3 illustrates the use of above stated technique. It shows how the process description emphasizes the most important aspects of the process:
- events and their consequences – process activities and states (i.e., points of waiting for the event),
- inputs and outputs processed by the process, including the main process' product (i.e. the main reason for the process run).

Note that this technique also answers the important question **"What is the proper level of granularity of the description?"**. The granularity level is given by the external factors influencing the process – by **events**). This concept states that there is just one activity between two states (i.e. events, consequently). This means that the eventual reason for the more detailed division of an activity is not objective any more. It must be subjective, because it is always relative to some other factor (technology, qualification, organization, etc.). In this way the technique identifies, on the other hand, the borders of possibility (i.e. making sense) in the optimization of a process.

4.3 THE PROCEDURE

Figure 4.4 expresses the procedure of the business processes system design as a set of succeeding/parallel steps:

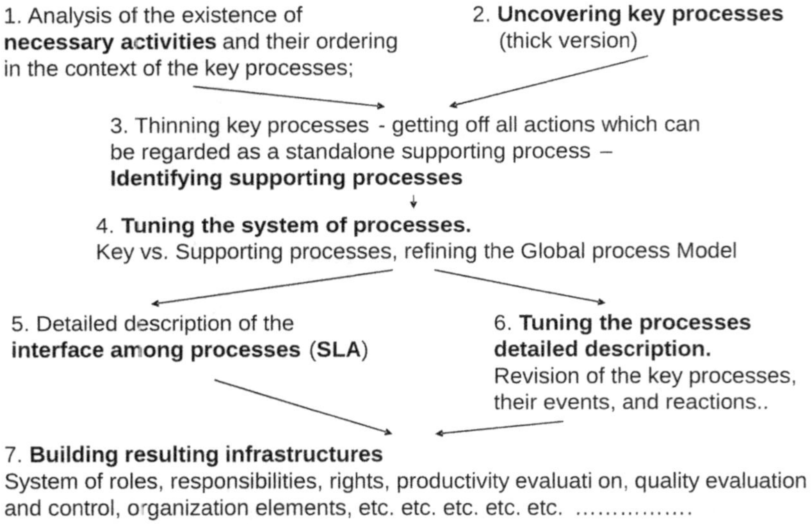

1. Analysis of the existence of **necessary activities** and their ordering in the context of the key processes;

2. **Uncovering key processes** (thick version)

3. Thinning key processes - getting off all actions which can be regarded as a standalone supporting process – **Identifying supporting processes**

4. **Tuning the system of processes.** Key vs. Supporting processes, refining the Global process Model

5. Detailed description of the **interface among processes (SLA)**

6. **Tuning the processes detailed description.** Revision of the key processes, their events, and reactions..

7. **Building resulting infrastructures** System of roles, responsibilities, rights, productivity evaluati on, quality evaluation and control, organization elements, etc. etc. etc. etc. ....

Figure 4.4. Procedure of the business processes system design.

In following paragraphs, some details of the particular steps are described.

STEP I: ANALYSIS OF THE EXISTENCE OF NECESSARY ACTIVITIES

In this step, the basic natural sequences of activities are revealed. The main subject of interest in this step is the natural succession of activities in the regular form as people know them, work flows, legal procedures etc. These sequences of activities serve in later steps as the basis for revealing the proper structure of the process system. Necessary activities (and their basic causal consequences) form the basis of the supporting processes. At the same time, they are the roots of the key processes as well. Thus the given set of natural activity sequences will be restructured in order to identify the key and supporting processes.

The outputs of this step are:
- List of potential processes/activities and their successions,
- first version of the process run models (basic process logic).

STEP 2: UNCOVERING THE KEY PROCESSES

The aim of this step is to show the key processes. Each key process represents, in fact, the way of achieving the key type of product. The structure of the key process can, thus, be derived from the life cycle of the key product, as a final result of the process. The key process is a process by which the organization realizes some external value – value for its customers.

In the example in Figure 4.2 it is obvious that the key product of the university is education. That means that the key process of the university is the education process, obviously. On the other hand, the key product of the university is obviously not the Study program accreditation as it does not realize any external value in itself – it rather helps the key process "education" to realize the value of education.

In the first version of the model, the key processes naturally contain a number of supporting activities and sub-processes (contextually). It is the important task for following steps to free key processes of all supporting activities (see below).

Main outputs of this step are:
- list of key processes and their relationships,
- basic attributes of the key processes,
- first version of the key process run models (basic process logic of the activities still containing a number of supporting activities which should be removed later).

Step 3: Thinning key processes

Every key process is naturally "long" because it covers the whole business case from the identification of the customer need till the satisfaction of this need by the product (service). As a result, the previous step has shown that the key processes are also "thick" – they contain a number of supporting activity chains. This step strives to remove, as much as possible, the supporting activities from the key processes. We are speaking about the "thinning" of the key processes.

All action chains which can be regarded as supporting chains arise from the key processes on the principle of "outsourcing" them into standalone supporting ones (even, possibly, outside the organization): any relatively standalone, continuous, homogeneous, and generalizable part of the process will be removed from the key process, generalized, and established as a supporting process. As a result of this removal some control activity (managing the supporting service delivery) remains in the key process in the original place of the removed supporting activity chain.

In the step 5, the interface to the original (mother) key process will be described including the basic parameters of the product/service (see the principle of SLA below).

The primary output of this step is the second version of the key process run models. They express the key process basic logic without the supporting activities. Secondary outputs are:
- actualized basic attributes of the key processes,
- a set of supporting processes newly discovered by removing supporting activity chains from the key processes.

Step 4: Tuning the system of processes

After thinning the key processes it is necessary to rework and elaborate models in detail, and complete the structure of the Global process model. In the previous step, new supporting processes were discovered, and the structure of each key process was simplified, consequently. The content, as well as the structure of the Global process model, has been changed and new interfaces among the processes have been created.

Main step outputs are:
- completed Global process model,
- completed specification of the interface among the processes (events, end states and their successions, and other important information for the SLA specification in the following step).

STEP 5: DETAILED DESCRIPTION OF THE INTERFACE AMONG PROCESSES

Interfaces among processes, which have arisen in the previous two steps, must be elaborated in detail. Great attention should be paid to the interface among key and supporting processes.

In this step, every interface is described in the form of "SLA" (Service Level Agreement). By the term SLA we mean an analogy to the Service Level Agreement widely used in outsourcing relationships. This form of agreement represents the universal view of any co-operation interface. This view is naturally compatible with the need for financial evaluation of services, building the system of productivity and quality metrics, etc.

The crucial meaning of the concept of services is explained in detail in the following section.

STEP 6: TUNING THE PROCESSES' DETAILED DESCRIPTION

Parallel to step 5, the revision of the key processes run, their events, reactions, and tuning of this description with the Global model, should be performed. Models are completed with actors, inputs, outputs; and overall revision of the Global model of processes is made in this step.

This step results in following outputs:
- actualized Global model of processes,
- actualized process attributes descriptions,
- actualized process run descriptions of the key processes and other important processes.

STEP 7: BUILDING THE RESULTING INFRASTRUCTURES

The final step of the procedure represents the interface to the subsequent activities of the organization building process. This step consists of the elaboration of the process interface in order to analyze the possibilities for realizing the service which the supporting process represents (the supplier part of the SLA).

Activities of this step lead to the creation of both main infrastructures:

- the basic requirements for the **organizational infrastructure** are analyzed with the definition of roles, their responsibilities, communication procedures, and other organizational aspects which follow on from the mutual competencies of both attendees of the business relation represented by the SLA;
- similarly, the **technical infrastructure** needs can be specified this way (necessary production and workflow technology support, as well as the necessary Information System services).

Particular outputs of this step are:

- Detailed specification of products/services from the SLA and their elaboration to the form of:
  - system of evaluation of the process' cost (cost-based price of the process product),
  - system of evaluation of the process' performance,
  - system of evaluation of the actors' performance,
  - outsourcing decision support system,
  - information requirements/needs of the processes,
  - and other managerial aspects of the organization...
- Casual detailed models of some supporting processes,
- etc.

4.4 Concept of Services

The conceptual model at Figure 4.5 shows the fragment of the universe of services in the context of business processes. It is necessary to distinguish between the Business Process Definition, and the Business Process Instance which represents the particular business process running in particular time with particular actors, inputs, outputs, etc. Each business process can collaborate with another process. The general view of the collaboration of processes is represented in this model with the Process Interface class as an association between two processes where the particular process has either the role of Supplier (producer of the Service) or Customer (consumer of the Service). In particular contact of particular processes the Process Interface has the role of the Contract template.

In general, the Business Process can be a Producer of one or more Services (see the direct association between Business Process Definition and Service).

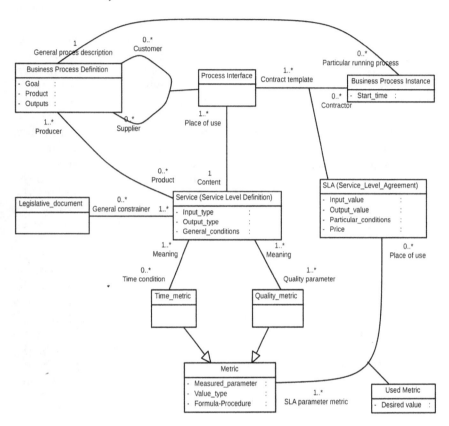

Figure 4.5. Process Services Conceptual Model

It is obvious that there must be the integrity constraint in the model which expresses the fact that there must exist direct association between the Business Process Definition and that Service which takes place within the Process Interface in which this business process exists in the role of Supplier. In other words, each business process must be the producer of all services which it supplies in various contracts.

The Service itself may be generally constrained by even more Legislative documents; it must have the association to at least one Quality metric, and it may be associated with one or more Time metrics. That means that there must always be some quantitative (measurable) notion of the quality of the service, and that some services also need to be time limited (what is the specific kind of the quality, in fact). Each service metric is characterized by the measured parameter, its value type, and the method of its gathering – formula or procedure

Every SLA should contain a product description (service characteristics, its meaning, value, sense), basic product parameters in measurable units, product quality metrics (how to measure quality as a general product attribute), and the product "price" which reflects the necessary costs of the supporting process or offered service.

The Service Level Agreement concretizes the general attributes of the Service with the particular attributes of the SLA; general Input is represented in the SLA by the Input data, Output by the Output data, General conditions of the service with the Particular conditions in the contract. SLA also contains the desired values of the metrics[11] of the service and the additional attribute – price of the service - which does not exist in the general view of the service. The price of the service always must be the result of the negotiation during the agreement specification and can never be stated as a general attribute of the service as it depends on many situational factors generally called the Market. By the way, this fact also illustrates well the crucial role of the outsourcing in the process-oriented management. In fact, such a description of the interface between two processes represents the real business agreement of these processes. It means that there is no difference between the "internal" and the real outsourcing (see Step 3 of the Procedure of the business processes system design above). Thus, this way of thinking perfectly prepares the situation for the possible outsourcing of all supporting processes where it is suitable.

4.5 CONSEQUENCES AND CONCLUSIONS

The methodology for business processes system design, presented in this chapter, which is based on the "principle of services", has been evaluated in several projects during the last four years. Every use of the methodology in the project brought some new experience and posi-

---

[11] See the association between the SLA and the Metric. It is obvious that even there (like in the case of relationships between Business Process Definition and Service), there must be the integrity constraint which expresses the fact that the metric values used in the SLA belong to the metrics generally associated to the Service.

tively influenced its content. That way, we finally uncovered the need for elaborating the concept of service in general, for instance. Projects covered the fields of university education, production, finance, and public administration. The main knowledge from this heterogeneous experience is:

- the idea of Process Management is valid in general, for all types of organizations, thus, it should not be reduced just to the area of market-oriented organizations;
- thinking in terms of services is relevant for all types of different systems harmonization: coordination of processes as well as harmonization of competences, following from the organization structure with specific process competences needed, harmonization of the organization specific needs with general technology possibilities, etc.;
- the traditional gap between the business conception and the applications' development can be overcome by regarding the so-called "user requirements" as services of the information system required by the nature of processes. This view of the problem also significantly changes the traditional approach to the distribution of tasks among typical roles in the information systems development, and, at the same time, explains the "role of the application user" often discussed nowadays in the communities of applications developers.

In this chapter we discuss the concept of services as a tool for Business Process Management. The text of this chapter just outlines some basic contingencies which follow on from the inspiration by the theory of services in the area of process management. It points out the significant similarities among different areas of the possible application of "service-oriented thinking", such as software development, process management, outsourcing, etc. It also points out the obvious convergence of all these phenomena – outsourcing as an original area of the SLA's is the principal way of recognizing the substantial differences between the key and supporting processes which, at the same time, directly corresponds to the need to tie the system of business processes in with the enterprise strategy on one hand, and with the supporting technology on the other hand.

The basic conclusion from the previous paragraph is: the concept of services should be regarded as a general principle for recognizing the interface between two substantially different areas connected with some common sense. This chapter shows how this concept works as a guide for specifying the interface between the various types of processes (key versus supporting ones), which differ mainly in the reasons and "speed", and are mutually asynchronous. It also shows how this principle can be used for specifying the interface between the system of processes and supporting infrastructures (technology as well as organization). A similar area of application of this principle is the interface between the strategic activities and process management of the organization which is not presented in this chapter. This interface is the main subject of the work of R. Kaplan and D. Norton (Kaplan, R. S., Norton, D. P. (2004)). Their theory could be also significantly extended this way.

In this chapter we have also described the basic procedure for analyzing and designing the system of business processes in the organization with respect to the consequential activities (building the resulting infrastructures). In this way, it outlines what should be an area of future development of the methodology.

5. Modeling Business Processes in Public Administration

5.1 Introduction

During the almost 20 years of its existence, business process modeling became a regular part of organization management practice. It is mostly regarded as a part of Information System development, or even as a way to implement some supporting technology (for instance, the work flow system). Although I do not agree with such a reduction of the real meaning of a business process, it is necessary to admit that information technology plays an essential role in business processes (see UML (2010) for more information). Consequently, an Information System is inseparable from a business process itself because it is a cornerstone of the general basic infrastructure of a business. This fact has an impact on all dimensions of business process management. One of these dimensions is the methodology that postulates that the Information System's development provides the business process management with the exact methods and tools for modeling the business processes. Also, the methodology underlying the approach presented in this chapter has its roots in the Information Systems' development methodology.

The field of public administration has, traditionally, interested researchers into the management theory. Unlike market-oriented businesses, this area poses considerably greater problems with its application of general management principles. The cause is, in particular, the absence of the market. This absence leads to the need for using a great deal of abstraction to implement those principles. Questions such as "Who is the customer?", or "What is the customer's interest?" are normally not easy to answer in this area[12]. The difficulty with using general management practices in this business can be seen, especially, in connection with business processes, namely with their reengineering. These problems manifest themselves specifically in identifying core processes.

The chapter is organized into two main sections. The first section deals with the topic of modeling business processes in general, regardless of the specific features of public administration. It explains the roots of the problem of modeling business processes, the basic principles, and the methodology used.

It also argues for a two-dimensional view of the "Real World". Specifically where attention is paid to the relationships between the two basic types of the "Real World" processes – on the one hand the processes of life cycles of real world classes, and on the other hand the business processes themselves.

The second section focuses on specific features of business process modeling in the field of public administration. It introduces the concept of Life Events, as it is frequently called, and emphasizes its close connection to the concept of Class Life Cycle, as well as its substantial role in the process of illuminating core processes in public administration. Because of the specific characteristics of the public administration area discussed above, this part of the chapter addresses the practices that are still infrequently applied in this field.

5.2 Life Events

The concept of *Life Events* is often used in the context of the process-oriented view of public administration. This concept represents the view of the natural consequences of public administration activities. These "natural consequences" are always given by the situation in the life of the public authority's "customer" – the *citizen*. And the life situations of a citizen are, in fact, very close to the main goal and objective reason for the public administration activities. It is obvious that such a view has very much to do with the main principle of business process reengineering – ordering activities according to the main goals, which have to be directly connected with the natural strategic

---

[12] For illustration, just try to answer these questions in the case of the process of the administration of criminal law. It is absurd to suppose that the perpetrator is a customer because his interest is diametrically opposed to that of the interest of the community (which is the real customer in this case).

goals of the organization – consequently, always following on from the *customers' needs*.

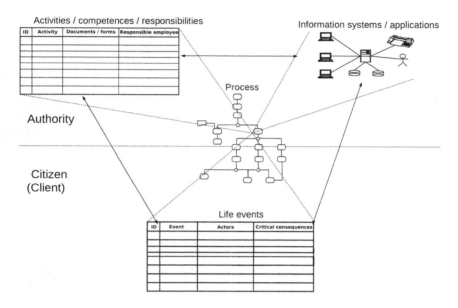

Figure 5.1. Different views of the public administration process.

Figure 5.1 illustrates the relationship between the most frequent views of the activities of the public authority[13]. It shows two different viewpoints:

- The point of view of the public authority typically emphasizes the "technical" aspects of the processes. Clerks usually look at their daily work in terms of individual activities, responsibilities and competences which are connected with their positions. Another, alternative, view from the same viewpoint is typical for the situation where the Authority owns a high-quality Information System – the daily work of each clerk is then viewable through the set of applications or sub-systems/databases.
- The point of view of the citizen represents quite a different approach. Nobody visits the Authority of his own free will. The citizen's visit is always caused by some problem, or situation –

---

[13] Note: This figure is just an illustration of the idea; the unreadable texts, as well as the process diagram are used as symbols and are not meaningful.

life event. The citizen typically does not care about the competences of the individual clerks, or Information Systems. The citizen has a problem which requires a solution.

Looking at public administration in terms of business processes
represents the third view which connects both different views discussed above. Such a view respects the technological aspects of the
administration (including legislation and organization of the Authority) as well as the needs of the customer (represented by the Citizen at
the Figure 5.1). Life events, thus, represent the needs (problems) of
citizens (customers in general), and trigger the administrative activities, all at once.

5.3 Deriving Life Events from Life Cycles of Crucial Classes

Life events became one of the most important subjects of
E-government's activities. There are several standard classifications of
life events as a reaction to the fact that standardization is very natural
in the area of public administration. These standards are of varying
quality – from simple descriptions of the routine activities of clerks, to
the lists of life events carefully analyzed as core representatives of public administration activities. One of the most interesting classifications
comes from the LEAP project.

LEAP (Life Events Access Project) is a partnership project between
British Councils. According to its mission statement "LEAP aims to
utilize knowledge management in order to improve service provision
to customers. The LEAP consortium will use new information and
communication technologies to develop services to best meet the
needs of customers and clients." In this project, life events are derived
from the conception of the standard life cycle of a citizen.

Figure 5.2 shows the simplified example of the Citizen life cycle description using the Statechart notation from UML (UML (2010)). The
example comes from the *Reference Public Administration Business Processes Model* project mentioned in the Conclusions. Each transition between the particular states is described by the triggering event together with the transition action. The transition action should correspond
to the action of some business process.

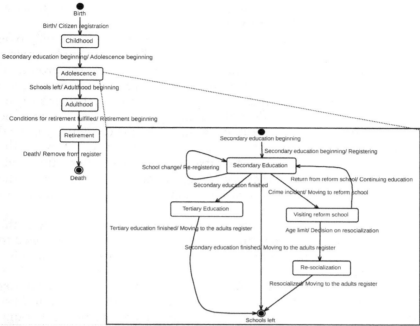

Figure 5.2. Example of the Citizen life cycle description.

It is obvious that such description of the object life cycle is a good basis for analyzing the crucial life events in order to constitute the interface between the authority and its customers.

5.4 DISCOVERING CORE PROCESSES FROM CRUCIAL LIFE EVENTS

According to the theory (Hammer M., Champy J. (1994), for instance), and the sense of business processes reengineering, core processes in the organization have to deal directly with customer needs[14]. Such a process always begins with the event representing the crucial need of the customer and ends with the satisfaction of this need.

As was stated in the previous section, life events represent important situations in the life of a citizen. It is obvious that ***crucial life***

---

[14] Original literature uses the term "customer requirements". Respecting the specifics of the public administration field, discussed above in the introduction, the term "customer needs" seems to be more suitable.

events should be candidates for the **triggers of** crucial business processes – *core processes of the Authority.*

As discussed above in the Introduction, *Citizen* is not the only type of the public authority "customer". Therefore, not only citizen-oriented life events should be taken into the account in the process of discovering core processes. For the most important processes, their "customer" is the community. As the main subject of the work of the Representation is the needs and requirements of the community, the primary "customer" of the Authority should be the community instead of the individual citizen. The global mission of the Authority (in the democratic political system, of course) is not just satisfying the needs of the individual, but, rather, satisfying the needs of all citizens – the community (in so far as possible respecting individual needs, of course).

To conclude from the previous paragraph, one can find that in the process of uncovering core processes of the authority, we also need to consider, besides the *citizen*, the events from the lives of some other objects. Typical objects, closely connected with fulfilling the needs of the community, are *Ground Plan, Financial Plan, Business Environment Development Plan*, and *Social Development Plan*. The life cycles of these objects address such events as "Request for change in the Ground Plan", "Investment intention", and "Social program proposal", etc. Such events seem to be the right candidates for triggers of core community processes.

Moreover, processes following on from the life events of the above mentioned objects are always in close connection with strategy-level decisions. Examples of such processes are: "Realization of the Change in the Ground Plan" or "Realization of the Social Development Action", etc. Such processes are not clearly processes of the authority, but, rather, the processes of the community because their key actors are not just clerks, but also community representatives and citizens.

On the other hand, there are also core processes whose triggers come from the life cycles of other objects existing in the area of public administration which are crucial, especially from the citizen's point of view. One example of all such objects is the *Construction* whose life cycle contains events playing important roles in core processes. In this case, it is the core process *House Building* with the supporting processes Planning *Permission* or *House Inspection* for example.

Discovering core processes from crucial life events, which is the subject of this section, thus requires at first **careful uncovering of the crucial classes,** and actors whose life events are the representatives of the core process triggers.

5.5 CONCLUSIONS

This chapter emphasizes the importance of modeling life cycles of objects as a natural complement to the business process description. It shows the practical significance of this two-way description of the "Real World" dynamics in the field of public administration processes and reveals the concept of *life events,* wide-spread in the area of E-government activities, to be a specific manifestation of the same approach. Life events are also identified as the right basis for revealing core processes in the field of public administration.

The theoretical parts of this chapter draw on the results of the project *OpenSoul.* The project is aimed at the development of the Business Processes Modeling Methodology based on the formal business process meta-model. For more information see OpenSoul (2000)).

Application of the theory in the field of public administration draws on the experience gained from the project *PARMA* (Public Administration Reference Model & Architecture) - see PARMA Project (2011). The project is aimed at the development of the general reference model of public authority processes and objects. Currently, the project is aimed at local authority processes where only the life events play the significant role.

REFERENCES

BPMN (2006) "Business Process Modeling Notation Specification", OMG Final Adopted Specification, February 2006, dtc/06-02-01 (http://www.bpmn.org/Documents/OMG Final Adopted BPMN 1-0 Spec 06-02-01.pdf).

Chen P. P. S. (1976) "The Entity Relationship Model – Towards a Unified View of Data", ACM TODS, Vol. 1 No. 1.

Coad P., Yourdon E. (1990) "Object-Oriented Analysis", Prentice-Hall Inc., NJ.

Eriksson, H. E., Penker, M. (2000) "Business Modeling with UML: Business Patterns at Work", Wiley.

Greenwood R. M., Robertson I., Snowdon R. A., Warboys B. C. (1995) "Active Models in Business", in Proceedings of 5th Conference on Business Information Technology BIT '95, Department of Business Information Technology, Manchester Metropolitan University.

Hammer M., Champy J. (1994) "Reengineering the Corporation: A Manifesto for Business Evolution", Harper Business, New York.

Jackson, M. A. (1975) "Principles of Program Design", Academic Press, London.

Jackson, M. A. (1982) "System Development", Prentice-Hall Inc., Englewood Cliffs, NJ.

Jackson, M. A. (2002) "JSP in Perspective"; in Software Pioneers: Contributions to Software Engineering; Manfred Broy, Ernst Denert eds; Springer.

Kaplan, R. S., Norton, D. P. (2004) "Strategy Maps: Converting Intangible Assets into Tangible Outcomes", Harvard Business School Press.

Kobryn, C. (2000) "Introduction to UML: Structural Modeling and
    Use Cases", Object Modeling with OMG – UML Tutorial
    Series: www.omg.org.
LEAP Project (2010) "Life Events Access Project"
    (http://www.lsbu.ac.uk/php4-cgiwrap/bcimsfsr/process-
    mapping/leap.php)
Lundeberg M., Goldkuhl G., Nilsson A. (1981) "Information Systems
    Development – A Systematic Approach", Prentice-Hall Inc.,
    Englewood Cliffs, NJ.
Marca, D., McGowan, C., IDEF (1992), "Business Process and
    Enterprise Modeling, Eclectic Solutions".
OpenSoul (2000) Repa, V.: "OpenSoul Project":
    http://opensoul.panrepa.org.
PARMA Project (2011): http://parma.vse.cz.
Repa V. (1995) "Hybrid development methodology", in Proceedings of
    5th Conference on Business Information Technology BIT '95,
    Department of Business Information Technology,
    Manchester Metropolitan University.
Repa V. (1996) "Object Life Cycle Modeling in the Client-Server
    Applications Development Using Structured Methodology",
    Proceedings of the ISD 96 International Conference, Sopot.
Repa V. (1998) „Methodology for Business Processes Analysis",
    Proceedings of the ISD 98 International Conference, Bled.
Repa V. (1999a) „Business Processes Based Information Systems
    Development", Proceedings of the BIS 99 International
    Conference, Springer Verlag, London.
Repa V. (1999b) "Information systems development methodology – the
    BPR challenge", Proceedings of the ISD99 International
    Conference, Kluwer Academics, Boise, ID, 1999.
Repa V. (200ca) "Process Diagram Technique for Business Processes
    Modeling", Proceedings of the ISD 2000 International
    Conference, Kluwer Academics, Kristiansand, Norway, 1999.
Repa V. (2003) "Business System Modeling Specification", In: Chu,
    Hsing-Wei; Ferrer, José; Nguyten, Tran; Yu, Yongquan (eds.).
    Proceedings of the CCCT2003 International Conference,
    IIIS, Orlando, FL, 2003.
Repa V., Matula M. (2002) "Business Processes Modeling with the
    UML", Research Paper, Prague University of Economics,
    Prague, Czech Republic, December 2002.
Repa, V. (2000b) "Business System Modeling Specification":
    http://opensoul.panrepa.org/metamodel.html.

Repa, V. (2004) "Business Processes and Objects in an Information Systems Development Methodology". In: Abramovicz, Witold (eds.). Business Information Systems – BIS 2004. Poznan.

Repa, V. (2007) "Modeling Dynamics in Conceptual Models". In: Advances in Information Systems Development, ISD 2006 Conference Proceedings, Budapest, New York : Springer.

Repa, V. (2008) "Process Dimension of Concepts". In: Jaakkola, H., Kiyoki, Y., Tokuda, T. Information Modeling and Knowledge Bases XIX. Amsterdam : IOS Press.

Rumbaugh J., Blaha M., Premerlani W., Eddy F., Lorensen W. (1991) "Object-Oriented Modeling and Design", Prentice-Hall Inc., Englewood Cliffs, NJ.

Scheer, A.–W. (1992) "Architecture of Integrated Information Systems – Foundations of Enterprise-Modeling", Berlin.

Scheer, A.–W. (1994) "Business Process Engineering – Reference Models for Industrial Enterprises", Berlin.

Turner, W.S., Langerhorst, R.P., Hice G.F., Eilers, H.B., Uijttenbroek, A.A. (1987) „SDM, System Development Methodology, North-Holland.

UML (2010) "Superstructure Specification", v. 2.3, document 2010-05-05. (http://www.omg.org/spec/UML/2.3/Infrastructure/PDF), Object Management Group.

Weisman, R. (1999) "Introduction to UML Based SW Development Process": www.softera.com.

Yourdon, E. (1989) "Modern Structured Analysis", Prentice-Hall Inc., Englewood Cliffs, NJ.

www.ingramcontent.com/pod-product-compliance
Lightning Source LLC
Chambersburg PA
CBHW030942070326
40689CB00042B/1478